KWA HERI

BLACK
DAUGHTER

by
Gisa Margarete Zigan

A BANTAM PREMIUM BOOK

INTRODUCTION

The following story is a factual, unsolicited account of one German family's moving experience in visiting their sponsored child in Kenya. An unanticipated opportunity allowed the family to travel to Africa and visit their sponsored child in a remote Kenyan village.

The simple style of the writer, telling the story through the eyes of the 10-year-old daughter, Mareike, provides the book with sincerity and integrity. The intensity of the feelings it portrays makes the story into one of genuine human interest, and provides a personal warmth that for both the family and the reader overcomes all the difficulties encountered in the journey.

But this is not only the story of one family's experience. The letters and messages that cross my desk from hundreds of sponsors who have made such journeys, some with and many without having first asked for our help in planning it, contain similar expressions of satisfaction. Almost without exception, the universal response of the sponsors has been one of profound satisfaction with the experience of encountering firsthand the child to whom they have been writing—and seeing the child in the context of the family or community where he or she lives. Many have described it as a transforming experience that they will never forget.

The first time that I visited one of the children we sponsor, I was very touched by the unreserved way in which he and his family welcomed me into their home and their lives. The unbounded generosity from those who seemed to have so little was disarming in its genuineness. Their friendship was warm and cordial. I was not an outsider but an instant member of the family and a close friend. No wonder so many say that the experience of meeting their sponsored child was one of the great moments of their lives.

There is one dimension to the story that I want to underline because it was so much a part of my experience as well. The concept of sponsorship links one individual to one child; but it never seems to work out that way. Sponsorship, in this story, was a family commitment in which all of the members of the family shared. And, when they arrived at the village in Kenya, they were received by the whole village and the sponsored child's family, as well as the child, Alice, herself. Sponsorship, at its best, is a bridge which brings individuals, families and communities together in a shared experience that transcends cultures and language.

The story contains a strong statement which says: "For those who can, one of the most meaningful and rewarding experiences you will ever have is to take the time to visit your sponsored child." And, for those who cannot make the trip, this story is a means by which you can vicariously share in that experience.

We did not solicit this story. The book came to our attention only after it had been published. It was the desire of the family to share their experience with others. We take this opportunity to send a copy to you for the same reason. You have graciously supported the work of the Christian Children's Fund. We invite you to read this story of another family's experience and pass it along to a friend. Collectively we are working to build a world-wide network of friendships which will be a force for good. One of the best ways of making the world better is by guaranteeing the best future possible for children who will be the leaders in the next generation.

God bless you.

Paul F. McCleary
Executive Director, CCF

"That's just a lot of lies!" Mr. Meierbrink's voice was getting louder and louder. But Mother did not lose her composure.

"We have all this proof. Look at it. The letters, the report from last semester, and now the report from the Christmas season."

She spread a stack of papers on the large dining room table at which she was sitting with Father, Mr. Meierbrink, and Mrs. Meierbrink, his fat wife.

Mareike was huddled on the large TV chair in the corner, and no one was paying any attention to her. She was still very little, only ten years old, and she should actually have been in bed long ago. There was no TV that evening, of course, since the Meierbrinks were visiting.

"We've got to finally get even with them," Mother had said, and Mareike had feared the worst. "Getting even" was something you did to your opponents after they'd beaten you in a fight or a game. But Mother explained, "This year they invited us to their garden party and to Mr. Meierbrink's fiftieth birthday. Now it's our turn to invite them and to show our hospitality." At seven o'clock they had come over from their home only a few houses away, and at first everything had been very peaceful and friendly because everyone was busy eating and drinking. Mother had placed cold roast and potato salad on the table and the preserves she had made from the berries that the four of them had picked that summer.

"You may come down at about half past eight and get your share," she had promised the two children, "I can't clear anything before that—it would look nibbled-at."

Mareike's brother, Jochen, who was already fifteen, shrugged his shoulders, pooh-poohed her, and said, "Bah, preserves. That's for children. Sweet stuff just gives you pimples."

He had recently become very conscious of his appearance and got furious whenever Mareike touched the lotions and ointments he kept in the bathroom.

"Leave him alone," Mother would say with a smile. "He's entering puberty and is about to take social dancing lessons—so his skin has to be clear."

"Where do you enter puberty?" Mareike had asked, for she did know where the dancing school was. She had been taking gymnastics lessons there since she was six.

"You don't enter puberty, you just get there by and by," Mother had explained with a smile. Jochen had run out of the room then, saying rude things in a loud voice, but this time Mother let it pass.

"Puberty is the time when a child develops into an adult," Mother had declared. "The body changes and sometimes it causes problems."

"Oh, I know," Mareike had said, "that's when your breasts start growing. But pimples one could really do without."

Anyway, that evening while the Meierbrinks were visiting, she was glad she had not entered puberty—yet—and she had been looking forward to the preserves all evening. Upstairs in her little room she had checked the time repeatedly on the clock mounted in the belly of a plastic Mickey Mouse, and the hands hardly seemed to be moving. When it was finally 8:25, she ran downstairs and curtsied awkwardly to fat Mrs. Meierbrink, earning a loving look from Mother and a plateful of preserves.

Then, when the animated conversation got started, the adults completely forgot the little girl on the TV chair in a dark corner. But Mareike was listening and understood exactly what it was all about. It was about the godchild in Africa, as Mother always called her.

"It's all a trick," Mr. Meierbrink repeated, his voice growing louder. "Your money never reaches the Negroes."

"Africans," Father interjected. "Africans or Blacks is what they're called now. Negroes is offensive."

"OK, Blacks," Mr. Meierbrink said and suppressed a belch caused by the good meal. "It's true, they're black enough. And I have nothing against them—right, Hilde?" He was seeking support from his wife. "Only recently we pressed a five-mark bill in the hand of the young man who wanted to sell us a newspaper, just like that."

"That's right, and I didn't even want a newspaper," added his fat wife. "After all, we have the weekly review and the news roundup every morning, although that one is getting worse all the time, but when the nice young Negro—Black—rang our door and flashed his white teeth at me—they have fantastic teeth, really—I was touched and was reminded of the movies on TV. You know: where Karl-Heinz is always helping the Blacks, because it never rains and they have nothing to eat ..."

"There you are," Mother broke in. You always had to do that with Mrs. Meierbrink, otherwise she would never stop chattering. "So you understand why we decided to sponsor a child. With fifty marks a month you can ensure that a child has enough to eat in Africa—or in another part of the Third World—and has a roof over its head and clothes to attend school in."

Mareike remembered how her parents had explained this to them a year ago. "Look at this package with instant pudding," Mother had said, "it costs one mark fifty-seven, If we do without it and quickly pick a few berries in the garden, we can easily save fifty marks per month."

"We can't pick any berries now," Jochen had remarked coldly. "This is November."

"Oh, don't be so petty," Mother had replied. "So you'll just get an apple from the shelf in the basement. This is a matter of principle. If we—that includes you, too—give up something superfluous, we can make a child happy in Africa, and you even get a little sister or brother."

"Better there than here," Jochen had said, for he was always afraid that Mother and Father would have another baby which might then come into his room—if it was a boy, anyway. In his room there wasn't a free spot left for a crib or playpen. It was crammed full of car and airplane models standing on the shelves, hanging from the ceiling, lying on the floor, and covering his desk on which he was supposed to do his homework.

Mareike, who had almost fallen asleep on her

soft chair, was startled as Mr. Meierbrink began snorting again.

"You can be sure the fifty marks are waylaid somewhere, in the pockets of some bureaucratic asses." Mareike was surprised that Mother didn't object. Whenever *she* used such an expression she would always be admonished.

"And there isn't any child. That's just to touch your soft heart."

"But we even have a snapshot." Mother was also getting loud. "Heinz, where's the picture?"

Heinz was Mareike and Jochen's father. His real name was Heinrich, but Mother called him that only when they quarreled. "Heinrich, you make me shudder," she would say then, and that was supposed to come from the poet Goethe, whom Mareike already knew about.

"Heinz, where is Alice's photo?"

"I've pinned it on the wall upstairs in my room," Mareike squeaked from her chair, and the four adults turned to her in surprise.

"Why aren't you in bed yet?" Mother scolded. She was red in the face, but that was surely from the alcohol and the argument with Mr. Meierbrink. "Now hurry. But let me have the snapshot so I can prove that Alice exists."

"Well, of course," Mareike said. "Jochen, who knows English, is always writing her letters. And she answers."

"That can be a trick," fat Mrs. Meierbrink said in a shrill voice. "They've got someone sitting in the organization who thinks up touching stories. That's how they draw money out of people."

Saying nothing, Mareike ran upstairs to get the snapshot off the wall.

She looked at it every evening because she liked the big black eyes so much. She couldn't tell whether Alice, who was three years older than she, had a sad expression or a fearful one. She probably looked so serious because she hadn't enjoyed the photo-taking session. Mareike hated it too and always squinted her blue eyes when Father used a flash.

That evening it took her a long time to fall asleep. She had had too much preserves and she was mad—at the Meierbrinks. How could they make such claims. Alice wouldn't lie, after all.

Or, more precisely, the Organization that reported on Alice. Regularly, twice a year. A closely printed form reported everything about the development of the child, her work in school and at home. It sounded strange, of course, when it was mentioned every so often that Alice helped her mother carry water, but Father had explained that: water pipes like they had didn't exist in the African village where Alice lived. The place was called Migwani—Mareike remembered that despite her fatigue.

"And where do they get the water from?" she had asked her father, and he had admitted that he honestly didn't know. Probably from the river or the village well they all shared. He had even read that during great droughts the water was brought to these areas by the government in large tank trucks, and that it would then be rationed out to the people.

"Good heavens, how are you supposed to take showers then?" asked Jochen, who was paying much attention of late to personal cleanliness and careful grooming, and Mother had added one of her frequent reminders not to use too much water for washing hands or brushing teeth and to shut the faucet promptly. After that talk about the hard hauling of water in Migwani, Mareike had actually been careful about water a few times, but then she forgot.

What else did the reports say about Alice? That she was a diligent and good child in school, that she helped her mother in the field ... "You see, you see," their mother had said, and she did not have to finish the sentence, for they both knew what she meant.

There were always discussions about the fact that they should at least clean their own rooms since they were doing so little else to help. Mareike was grateful that her room was dark and so her bad conscience was not aroused by all the toys lying around. She would clean up tomorrow; she was quite determined to do that. The Meierbrinks would not be able to claim that she was lazier that her African godchild. But then the Meierbrinks did not even believe that such a child existed. She must be sure to ask her mother how the rest of the evening had gone when she came to kiss Mareike good night. She had to know whether the Meierbrinks had been persuaded by the snapshot and by Father's explanations, these silly ignoramuses who ... and then Mareike fell asleep.

By morning she had forgotten all about it, since breakfast and leaving for school were very hectic as usual. Jochen once again stayed too long in the bathroom which the two children had to share, and Mareike did not have enough time to do her own braid. Mother had to do it while Mareike crammed in her oat flakes, and Jochen had found that very unappetizing.

"Yech, combing at the breakfast table," he said with contempt, and Mareike reminded him for the thousandth time that it was his own fault—with his constant pimple pressing before the mirror. Before they could get into a fight, Father sounded his horn from the driveway, and they had to hurry out. He always took them along to the nearest subway station since they would otherwise have had to leave even earlier to get to the bus station, and the whole family wanted to sleep that extra quarter hour.

Actually, their father did not have to be at work that early. He was "independent," meaning that he could set his own working hours. But he did not mind rising early, or maybe he just pretended not to mind for the sake of the family.

"I can review the files in peace before going to court," he said, "and have it all fresh in mind when the action starts."

Mareike did the same before class. She would quickly read the material during recess so she could remember it all. Her father was a lawyer, and she always imagined how he would help suspects and defendants prove their innocence and remain free. A savior of the helpless, a modern Robin Hood. But his work was not really all that exciting. He sometimes described cases that involved boring contracts, division of assets, etc.; only rarely did he act as a criminal defense lawyer.

The morning went fast since it was Saturday and they had only four hours of school. They could have done without school, Mareike often thought with irritation. Other people were off on Saturday; only schoolchildren had to work. All right, not every Saturday, because the first Saturday of the month was free. And there was no real work today either, for they had two hours of art class with a young teacher who let them draw anything they wanted, then one hour of physical education, and finally geography, where they were shown a movie.

That's the way it was on most Saturdays; during the fourth hour, Miss Ruttlewski would show them a film.

"She's had enough too and is looking forward to the weekend with her boyfriend," Jochen, the oldest in the class, claimed with a smirk. He must be right, he had known her longer because he had had to repeat the fifth grade. "Voluntarily," he insisted.

Mareike and the others had only entered the secondary school in September, and they thought Miss Ruttlewski was really quite nice. Not only because she did not inflict difficult questions on them on Saturday but also because she was a lively, pretty, young woman. On Saturday she was always particularly elegant, wearing slacks, colorful sweaters, and tennis shoes. Mareike thought that she must play a lot of sports during the weekend, for she had seen tennis rackets and balls when Miss Ruttlewski jumped into her sporty coupe after school. She must surely be glad to move about at last after all the sitting in class.

Mareike understood that very well. She too always ran out like a wild deer when they were let out of school at last, just so she could stretch her legs.

At lunch time she remembered the Meierbrinks and Alice in Africa.

"How did it go last night?" she asked her mother, who still had some leftover preserves.

"Oh, quite well," Mother answered, and she reported that they would have liked to cut short the discussion about Alice and hunger in Africa because Mr. Meierbrink was getting so excited and they didn't want to spoil the evening.

"There's always a doubting Thomas," Mother said, and Mareike actually remembered the story from her religious instruction. The doubting Thomas was the one who believed only what he could see and touch. The story was about Jesus's resurrection, but it could also be applied to other things.

"We'll just have to bring Alice here, so she can be seen and touched," Mareike suggested, and felt very smart.

"How are you going to do that?" her brother objected immediately. He always criticized anytime she, the little one, suggested anything. "How are we supposed to get them out of the primeval forest?"

"There is no primeval forest in Kenya," Mother pointed out with a gentle smile. "You should know that from the letters and reports. Most of it is dry grassland, and that's precisely the problem."

Jochen blushed and growled that he had simply meant Alice would be hard to find in the wilderness.

"You talk like the Meierbrinks," Mareike exclaimed. "After all, we have the address where we send all our letters."

"That's a post box in Nairobi, the capital," Jochen informed her, having retrieved his self-respect. "You don't think Alice lives in a post box, do you?"

Mareike could not imagine that either and looked to her mother for support.

"We know a little more than that," said Mother. "We know the name of the village where Alice lives with her large family. The post box simply belongs to the Organization, which forwards our letters and contributions."

Were the Meierbrinks right after all? Mareike

asked herself. After all, a name was easy to propose or invent. It was true that they never got any mail directly from Alice. It always came via the Organization's office, always the same sheets of blue paper with English-language messages written in capital letters.

Her thoughts were interrupted by Father, who had finally arrived for lunch. He had had to "study some cases," as he would say, and in her mind's eye Mareike saw him moving mounds of paper and files around.

She remembered that she had wanted to clean up today, and when she announced her decision, Mother looked at her with pleasure.

"May I then look through the file with the letters and reports from Africa?" Mareike asked, knowing that she'd get permission.

"You don't understand it anyway," Jochen said disparagingly. Mareike, who had been studying English for eight weeks, kicked him in the shins.

But the cleaning took more than two hours, and before opening the file Mareike had to fortify herself with a soft drink and some of the cake that Mother always baked on weekends.

She had her own desk, which now looked large and empty—one could not tell immediately that many things had simply been squeezed into the drawers—and she was able to spread out all the papers so they would be easy to study. In the middle, she placed the gray-and-white Polaroid snapshot showing the serious, almost sad face of a child with huge dark eyes and short-cropped, tightly curled hair.

There was also a form with information about the child:

Name: Alice Ilai, No. 630230/00128
Migwani Family Helper Project
Sex: female
Date of Birth: 1975

Even with only her first-year English she understood that. Help was being given to families in
Migwani, including the Ilai family. About the word
"sex" she had not known at first whether to giggle
or feel embarrassed, but Jochen, her clever brother,
had nonchalantly explained it simply meant whether the child was a boy or a girl, i.e., female, and he
had commented that it was typical of immature
ten-year-old girls always to think certain things.

"I don't do that at all," Mareike had hissed
back at him. "Who tells you such nonsense in the
subway? The ninth-graders?"

"Just don't listen if you don't like them," Jochen
said crossly. "And anyway, what does this have to do
with me? I'm not responsible for the stupidity of
the other guys."

They had all wondered why Alice's date of
birth was not given.

"Must be an oversight," Father said. "I'll call
the German branch of the Organization."

He made a special long-distance call to Southern Germany because they all wanted to know the
date of birth so they could send Alice a nice present. But his telephone conversation was a disappointment. That's the way it often is in Kenya, they
told him; there were so many children, often a
dozen or more per family. They simply didn't record
the date of yet another birth. And most of the
people were illiterate anyway; they couldn't read or
write. How were they to know what date it was?"

True, they said, to be sure this child, Alice, was going to school and was learning these things—like many other children, now that schooling was mandatory—but when the kids had nothing to wear or were needed in the fields, they simply skipped school. That is why they were so grateful to the godparents in Germany for their contributions. They made it possible to buy clothes for school and food in the event of another emergency.

"Fantastic," Jochen said when Father explained all this. "I would love to skip school whenever I can't find anything to wear."

"Me too," Mareike agreed, because she hated the long way to school and the subway ride. "I'd also rather stay at home."

"What strange ideas you have," Father said, and he was undoubtedly tempted to start giving a lecture on how different living conditions were in Africa, but they had often discussed this before becoming godparents. Now he wanted to say something about Alice's birthday.

"Well, we could set a birthday ourselves," the lady from the Organization said, "but we can't send any presents."

"But why not?" Mareike cried in disappointment. She dearly loved to wrap presents and was the one who did it for the whole family. Whenever grandparents, godmothers, or friends had to be remembered, Mother would entrust the present to Mareike for wrapping. The lady had said that customs officials asked so much money for foreign packages that the Organization could not afford it, nor could the godchildren's families, of course. But the godparents were free to make an additional contribution, over and above the fifty marks each month, and Alice could then use that money to buy herself anything she wanted. About thirty marks would seem appropriate.

"Thirty marks"—Mother looked at her children—"that's barely enough for a sweater."

"Alice would have little use for a pullover in Africa," Father said drily. "Just leave it to the people down there."

Among the papers on her desk, Mareike had found an acknowledgment that the birthday money had been received. Attached was a short thank-you note from Alice. Mareike remembered that Alice had used the money to buy shoes for herself and for her mother, and Mareike recognized the English word "shoes." At the time, about half a year ago, she had been a little upset that Alice hadn't used it all for herself, but her parents had commented, "Maybe that's precisely what gave her pleasure, to give pleasure to someone else."

Did Alice have any toys? Of course—there were dolls everywhere in the world. She could make one herself, or her father could whittle one for her.

Mareike examined the photos illustrating a brochure about Kenya. They showed slender Blacks minding herds of cattle, little houses with thatched roofs, young girls knitting together in one room. And there were also views of high-rises in Nairobi and the white sand of Indian Ocean beaches. Despite the illustrations and the descriptions, she could not really picture Alice's surroundings. On the one hand, her living conditions were so primitive that she had to fetch water every day. On the other hand, she could buy shoes if had the money. Could someone also send her money for a water conduit? Mareike ran down to ask her parents, who were just getting dressed to go out.

"I'm not that rich," her father laughed while putting on an elegant red tie. "A water supply system for a village in the grasslands is a major project. That would have to be done by the government."

"And the government is doing it, too," Mareike's mother added. "There are fertile and cultivated regions in Kenya, but it is a huge territory and Alice happens to live way out in the country."

"Mareike, 'You Bet' is just starting," her brother called from the living room, and Mareike forgot all about Africa's water problems.

"Bye-bye, you two," their parents shouted from the front door. "Enjoy your TV program."

Their parents were lenient on weekends. On weekdays Mareike had to be in bed by eight, and Jochen no later than ten, and no moaning or pleading would help. But tonight he could watch TV till eleven, first "You Bet" with Thomas Gottschalk, then sports. By 9:30 Mareike was already dog-tired and announced, "I'm going to bed," whereupon Jochen immediately asked, "Would you please give Lollipop his milk?"

He asks so nicely because he doesn't want to miss any of the program, Mareike thought, but she didn't mind feeding the fat tomcat. Lollipop got a saucer of diluted warm milk every evening, although they were always reading that milk was not good for cats. "Nonsense," Father would say. "When I was growing up in the country every cat got milk."

And Lollipop seemed to thrive on it. He was fat, of course, and pink skin showed through the white hair on his belly, but he was still quite agile for his seven years and could climb any tree in the garden. Lollipop was the name Jochen had given him when they adopted the foundling kitten seven years ago. He apparently had run away or been chased away from his mother too early, because he would still suck fingers like a little baby whenever he found a hand to lick.

A permanent sucker one of the parents had called him, and Jochen immediately found the right name: Lollipop.

Even now he still had this habit when he was sleepy and purring, but no one in the family really liked it. It would tickle when he sucked and licked a finger with his pink-white little mouth.

"Here is your evening milk, Mr. Lolli," Mareike called to the cat, and she watched him while he drank in the kitchen.

"Have a good sleep and go to your basket in the hallway."

But she knew that Lolli would go there only when all the doors were closed and all the soft spots were beyond his reach. If they didn't watch out he would suddenly be in the bed or in the laundry basket or on the TV chair. He loved to sleep on the cushions of the patio chairs, but only in summer. Right now it was much too cold outside, and the cushions were in the basement.

Mareike was so tired that she just managed to brush her teeth and rinse her face before dropping into bed like a log. She forgot all about Thomas Gottschalk and Lollipop and Alice in Africa, and if she were to dream of them, she would not remember in the morning anyway.

Breakfast was late the next morning, and the tomcat was very displeased that he was not allowed into the garden until so late. He whipped his tail and made big yellow eyes.

When Mother sleepily opened the door for him, he was outside with a leap—but was back in a minute. "Too cold for you, Lolli?" Mother asked as she gave him his breakfast. No sweet rolls like the children, of course; just cat food out of the can. And Lolli would have loved to taste some of the sweet rolls; he made that quite clear by rubbing against their legs.

Mareike sat at her desk all Sunday and switched back and forth between her school books—she was supposed to write two papers that week—and the documents about Alice. At some point Lollipop had entered the room and was now spreading himself all over the desk. He loved to lie on soft paper. But when he started playing with it and his claws made holes in one of the sheets, Mareike shoved him onto the floor.

"Shoo, tomcat," she said, but not too loud—he didn't like that. "You have no feeling for culture."

Did they have cats in Africa? Lions, yes, of course. She knew that from books and movies. But domestic cats? She would have to tell Jochen to ask Alice in his next letter.

The following weeks were not particularly pleasant. It was rainy and stormy. "Typical November weather," Father commented, and on several occasions he drove the children all the way to school instead of just to the subway station, because Mareike easily caught colds.

The eager beavers submitted one paper after another. "They always do that," Jochen said. "They want to have everything done by Christmas so they can go skiing."

Mareike had been used to more of a Christmas atmosphere in elementary school, but she managed the work load and did not find it really difficult. I would like to go skiing, too, she often thought as she looked at the gray sky, but their parents explained that they still owed a lot of money on the house they had bought only three years ago.

Up to then, they had lived in a rental house nearby, and naturally it was much nicer to be in their own home with a garden, no matter how small. At the start, Lolli had been afraid to go outdoors and had first carefully tested the green grass with one fat paw. But he was soon running around for hours on end, and their neighbor sometimes complained that he chased her birds away.

"If only he had remained a house cat and were afraid of the outdoors," Mother sighed sometimes, and she assured Mrs. Hoerdelmann, their neighbor, that her cat would certainly never catch any birds. Mother had once quickly and secretly removed a dead thrush from the patio, but Jochen, who saw that Mother was upset and that Mareike was stricken, had said, "It must have been sick and broken-winged, otherwise he would not have caught it. You should be thankful that he put an end to its suffering."

"I hope that's really the way it was," Mother said, and cast a cold look at Lolli. "He's restricted to quarters for the day, anyway."

On the first day of Advent, when they drove to visit their grandparents, it still wasn't snowing. Mother had bought a poinsettia, a large potted plant, and Mareike had decorated the pot with an artful sheath of silver paper.

At the front door of their grandparents' little house, they were met by a delicious aroma of cinnamon and apples. Granny had been baking, you could smell it. "Wonderful," Father proclaimed, "just like when I was a young."

He had grown up here and still felt very much at home in his parents' small-town house. Mother agreed with him, but she had once said, "Well, I wouldn't like to live there forever."

She had grown up in a large city in Northern Germany, and until Jochen was born she had worked in the office of a large company.

"I need life, and people, and the city," she admitted. "In a little town, where everybody knows everybody, I'd feel cooped up."

That afternoon at their grandparents' was very comfortable, undoubtedly because they were full of apple pie and almond cookies. The children listened quietly to the long stories about the good old days when everything was better, more orderly, and cheaper. Both of them were already thinking of Christmas. After all, the red candle burning on the table announced that coming event. When their grandparents finally asked what the children wanted for Christmas, Mareike grabbed all her courage and asked, "Couldn't you, when you give us books for Christmas ..." She paused and timidly glanced at Grandma to make sure she didn't mind, but Grandma was sipping liqueur and smiling, "... couldn't you make it a gift certificate? We do get so many things, and we might get the same thing twice..."

"And besides, you want more exciting books than the ones we select, right?" Grandpa interrupted and laughed as she blushed. "Your dear mother has already given us a hint. I fully understand. You aren't little children anymore."

On the way home Jochen gratefully said to his

sister, "You did that very well. I wouldn't have dared, but I don't want to receive my twentieth volume of Karl May either." (Karl May is every German child's favorite writer on the American West.)

The weeks before Christmas went by much too fast. There was so much to do in school and at the desk at home, and the stores got more crowded all the time, making shopping tiresome. The whole family was nervous, and they breathed easy only on the last Advent Sunday when it snowed.

Lolli came in from the garden deeply offended and shook the snowflakes from his gray-striped back. He did not like cold and humidity, and vented his anger at the Advent wreath by pulling at its red bow.

"Next time, I'll hang it from the ceiling," Mother promised herself, "so the darn cat can't reach it."

"He'll just jump for it," Jochen predicted.

"That would be good for his fat belly," she said without pity. "A little exercise would do him good."

"Why don't we decorate an extra Christmas tree, just for Lolli," Mareike proposed, "with little goodies he could pluck for himself?"

"What kind of goodies?" Jochen asked. "Sausage and dead mice?"

"Gold sardines, maybe," Mareike mused.

But Mother protested, "Can you imagine the mess? Shredded sardines under the Christmas tree!"

The children giggled at the idea of the funny scene.

"Would be something different," Jochen said.

"Some of the kids in my class don't celebrate Christmas at home," Mareike told them. "They take off on ski vacations." She was a little envious of those lucky kids, but she wouldn't admit it.

But Mother must have sensed it, because she

said consolingly, "You'll do that too, someday, when the mortgage on the house had been reduced a little."

Mareike often felt quite lonely in her class, and that was probably why she would gaze every evening at the snapshot of Alice in Africa and try to picture how she lived and what she did in school. She knew from the reports that Alice had to learn English, too, since her mother tongue was Kikamba. She belonged to the Akamba tribe, and at home they spoke differently than in the schools and offices. That happened in Germany, too. Some children speak Low German or Bavarian dialect with their parents, and in school they must get used to High German, which is understood throughout Germany. Alice also took mathematics and physical education, but did she learn anything about Germany in her geography classes? It was so far away and so tiny, compared to Africa.

Mareike often tried to imagine before falling asleep what would happen if she were to bring Alice to school with her. The others would be amazed that she had a "Black sister," and they would fight to sit next to her. Could Alice possibly come to Germany someday? Just for a visit? But Mareike didn't mention this to anyone, fearing that Jochen would laugh at her and that their parents would again list all the money they still owed. But it certainly would be neat ...

Mareike and Jochen made a last shopping tour in town together. They still did not know what to bring their grandparents when they visited them on Christmas Day. Mareike did have a whole stack of nice drawings from which she would have to select just one, but Jochen thought that wasn't enough. Besides, she had drawn palms and Black Africans and giraffes on many of the pages, and she wasn't really sure their grandparents would like them all that much.

Jochen had an idea. "You know what, let's just buy a picture frame. Mother always brings them so many photos of us and the house. They could hang one of them on the wall."

"That's a good idea," said Mareike. "Maybe they'll frame one of Lolli, like the one Mother has over the kitchen table."

They searched in the department store for a long time among the wooden and metal frames and finally picked one made of a thin gold strip.

"That looks very elegant and solid," Mareike said. "Grandma likes that."

For their parents they had both already bought things some time ago. Father was to get a handbook on gardening, because he often announced how he was going to transform the garden and create a "green paradise." Up to now he had only mowed the lawn—and even that only when Mother reminded him reproachfully. They had planted all the shrubs and bushes, and the children had helped a few times with the weeding. But that, too, was done only just before Mother's Day or Mother's birthday in August. Maybe this book would motivate Father to become an enthusiastic gardener.

"One must try to educate one's parents," Jochen commented. "It's good for the whole family,"

For Mother they had no educational plans, but they did hope they were responding to a secret wish. They had bought for her a "Golden Oldies" album because she had every so often expressed nostalgia for the Rock'n Roll era.

Mareike spent the hours before Christmas Eve at her desk, wrapping, tying, and decorating all the gifts. Jochen went with Father to buy the Christmas tree, and he helped him cut the trunk and screw it into the stand.

Mother was in the kitchen almost all the time, and terribly nervous. The tomcat sat with wounded pride in the hallway before the closed door and tried to call attention to himself by wailing resentfully. Nobody would play with him; nobody petted him. What was going on here?

Lunch on December 24th was simple, as usual. There was only herring and potatoes—to leave room for all the delicacies they would have that evening.

In the afternoon, the children went to church with Mother while Father decorated the tree. Mareike had suspected for some time that that was only an excuse because he wanted to get out of going to church, but then she wasn't any better herself. They rarely went to church—at Christmas, of course, and for the harvest festival, and they were all grateful when Father gave them excuses.

"The churchgoers are not always the best people," he said. "One can also worship at one's workplace or in nature."

Today, on the afternoon of December 24th, the church was crowded, as always for Christmas. Mareike enjoyed the warmth, the candle glow and the singing of the congregation. It would not have taken very much more to make her cry. Mother looked very serious, like all the others. But actually this was wrong, as Jochen explained for the nth time on the way home:

"This is a cheerful festival, a joyful celebration," he said. "Why do the people look so sad? Our English teacher told us that in England people laugh and dance on this day. The rooms are decorated with garlands and anyone may get kissed under the mistletoe hanging in the door frame."

"That's the way I would like to celebrate someday," Mareike said. But when they waited on the other side of the door to the living room where Father was decorating the tree, they got caught up in the festive mood. A little bell rang inside and Father called for them to come in, and they could finally admire the decorated Christmas tree.

It was a great moment, like every year. The honey candles spread their sweet scent, the little tinsel angels turned silently among the branches. As usual they were all supposed to sing "Oh, Christmas Tree" together, but Jochen reminded them his voice was breaking and he hummed softly. Father couldn't really sing anyway, and so it was up to Mother and Mareike to sing high and loud and clear. But after the second verse they stopped and rushed to open their presents.

Mareike had received everything on her wish list and, in addition, the kind of stylish pullover considered "in" at her school. It was not inexpensive, she knew, because the Italian manufacturer's name was displayed on it in large characters, and actually Mother considered this to be awful. That is why Mareike was particularly grateful to Mother because she would now be able to hold her own with her classmates, and she turned around to Mother to tell her that.

Mother was standing like a statue with her mouth wide open next to the Christmas tree and was staring at the letter she held in her hand.

"Heinz," she stammered, her voice sounding strange and thin. "Heinz, Jochen, Mareike, listen to this. Aunt Hedwig sent us a check for ten thousand marks!"

"I don't believe it!" Father and Jochen cried in one voice, but Mareike said nothing.

"But it's true. She sold her house and wants to enter a home for the elderly, and that's why she is giving away part of her money."

Mareike reviewed in a flash what she knew about Aunt Hedwig. She lived alone in a house full of pictures and stuff—long ago she had a husband, but no children. Aunt Hedwig painted pictures and wrote little poems, but she did not like to visit or write long letters. She was a strange and reclusive lady, Mother would always say of her. And now this amazing news.

"She wants to give it away while her hands are still warm," Mother read aloud.

Since Mareike seemed not to understand, Jochen explained, "It means while she's still alive. After all, most people's inheritance gifts are granted after their death."

"Don't be so cynical," said Mother. "But you are right, in fact. Good heavens, I certainly never expected this! I did write to her from time to time, and this Christmas I sent her a snapshot of you kids, but the thought that she would give us ..."

"Why us?" Father wondered. "She has other relatives, after all."

"Yes, a distant cousin of mine is getting the same amount," replied Mother, "and some friends are also receiving money. 'The rest,' she writes, 'I need to buy membership in this posh retirement home and to pay for my monthly rent and meals.

Fortunately, I can keep my parrot. Otherwise I wouldn't go there, despite my eighty-three years. But I find it increasingly hard to do the shopping and housekeeping. Do whatever you want with the money. And for the rest, Merry Christmas.'"

Well, this was indeed a merry Christmas. So much money out of a clear blue sky! There was so much one could buy and pay for for which Father's income wouldn't suffice.

Mareike expected her father to say something to that effect, but looking very youthful despite his forty years, he suddenly exclaimed: "I think we should indulge in something quite crazy ..."

"We could fly to Miami!" Jochen suggested excitedly. He had been bitterly disappointed to discover the day before that his favorite program, "Miami Vice," would not be broadcast because of the holidays.

"Or go skiing in the Alps," proposed Mareike.

"Or buy Mother her own car at long last," said Father, who liked to spoil his wife but just wasn't a rich man.

"You know what?" Mother straightened out next to the Christmas tree so she was almost as tall as the tree and was lit by all the candles, "We're going to Africa."

"To Africa," squeaked Jochen, whose voice really broke this time.

"To Africa," repeated Mareike softly, while Father looked lovingly at his wife and said in a low voice, "Vera, you're crazy, but that's why I love you. Why not Africa?"

That's how fast things went that evening, but the following weeks were to show that it wasn't all as simple as it had seemed to them on that lovely, radiant Christmas Eve. First of all, there had to be a big argument with their grandparents. At the beginning of the holidays they drove like every other year to the little town where Father grew up. They were actually full of the good meal and weren't as eager as usual for Grandma's cake.

Lolli, too, was sated and content—Mareike had added a large portion of turkey roast to his normal meal. He lay in the hallway basket and barely pricked his ears when the children called out, "Bye-bye, cat."

But in grandparents' cozy narrow living room with the tree trimmed white and silver, they felt the Christmas spirit and were full of anticipation. Here, too, there were presents on the table. Jochen was delighted to find, instead of volume No. 20 of Karl May's works, a little pouch of "pieces of silver" which he could use to buy anything he wanted. Mareike also discovered some of the coins in the heavily lined gloves that looked like real skiing gloves, not like children's mittens. She therefore accepted with serenity Grandma's other present, Mickey Mouse handkerchiefs, which she would never use in class.

Everything was pleasant and peaceful until Father burst out with, "We are going to Africa this summer."

"Is that the beginning of a joke you're about to tell us?" asked Grandpa, and his wife peered with wonder at Heinz, her grown son.

"Not at all. Vera, my golden dove"—Father was to use that name often in the days to come—"my golden Vera was given ten thousand marks as a present."

"Who from?" The old couple looked at her with amazement, and almost a little suspicion.

So Mother told them about Aunt Hedwig, her lonely but original way of life, and about her decision to give away everything superfluous and to retire to a home for the elderly.

"And she simply gave you ten thousand marks?" Grandpa, who had spent his adult life as a frugal civil servant, still couldn't grasp the whole thing. "You could pay a good portion of the mortgage."

"That's precisely what we don't want to do," his son Heinz said calmly. "We are going to use the money to visit Africa."

"And to visit Alice, our African child," added Mareike.

This had been immediately clear to them on Christmas Eve when Mother mentioned Africa, but the reason had to be stated again to the grandparents.

"You've gone off the deep end," Grandfather grumbled, ignoring the Christmas mood and Grandma's bewildered look.

"All that money. You can't just throw it out the window like that."

"That's not what we're doing," Mother intervened very calmly. "We want to take a long journey to show the children something of the world and to get to know the child for whom we have assumed responsibility."

"Balderdash"—Grandpa was really getting overwrought today—"they can see enough of the world when they're grown-up. In all my life I never got further than Austria and Russia."

"Yes," said Father, "and Russia wasn't even a voluntary visit, because you went as a soldier. We want our children to travel early in their lives—and for other reasons."

"And anyway, your Black child," Grandma now joined the discussion, "what does that mean? Who knows whether she really exists."

"You talk like the Meierbrinks!" exclaimed Mareike, and the whole sorry discussion started all over again. The candles burned down, their seats got clammy in the warm room, and the festive mood was over.

In the course of the following weeks the four of them realized that the grandparents' attitude was not an exception. Whenever the planned trip to Africa was broached—which happened infrequently, but still a few times when meeting with friends and acquaintances—the initial reaction was surprise, amazement, incomprehension.

"To throw away so much money in two or three weeks, what a shame!" was the reaction.

And when Father pointed out that some families spend that much money for one foreign trip and buy a new car every two years—his was seven years old—the response was, "Yes, but those people do not owe money on their home and don't have children still going to school."

Father could have commented on that, for there were many cases in the files of his law firm of people who were spending too much because they wanted to have everything at once. These people accumulated debts, had to declare bankruptcy, or even got swept into criminal acts. But as an attorney he was sworn to secrecy, just like a physician, and besides, his own case did not compare in any way.

"It's simply a lucky break," he said again and

again, "unexpected and unplanned, just like winning the lottery. We should use it for something special. Our daily life is well planned and secure. For that, we don't need Aunt Hedwig's money."

To tell the truth: in the privacy of the family they did still discuss whether the trip to Africa was really the best they could do with the money. Jochen even once more proposed Miami in America as a destination.

But Mother remained steadfast. "This is my aunt and my present, and I know it will be good for all of us to take this trip. And for Alice, too."

She continued, "We are going to Kenya and we will see for ourselves whether the Organization is helping our Alice and the other children there. Jochen will bring his camera and take pictures, and I will write a letter now announcing our visit." She also wrote a letter to Aunt Hedwig describing her plans. That answer came quickly; the one from Africa took weeks.

Aunt Hedwig was enthusiastic about her niece's project and even gave a little encouragement: "Do go to Kitui in Africa and visit places never seen before."

Kitui was the province where the village Migwani was located and where Alice lived. Naturally, Mother's letter had again gone to the Organization's post box in Nairobi, since the little girl did not have her own address.

Weeks passed, and nothing came. Jochen was distracted because his social dancing classes had finally started. His skin was long since clear, and he even got some elegant slacks and a striped shirt. Actually he would have liked even more expensive things, and he pouted, "But we got so much money from Aunt Hedwig."

Mother stuck to her guns and reminded him of their vacation project.

"For the final ball you can choose yourself a sharp blazer," she promised. "Right now you're looking good enough."

Mareike thought so too. She was always amazed when her brother left for his dance class on Friday afternoon. He seemed so tall to her, almost a grown-up. Not at all like one of the rowdy ninth-grade students they met in the subway every morning.

She hadn't said anything yet in class about her project or about Alice, for she still had no close friend. Mareike was not unpopular—she sensed that. But most of the other kids had come in groups from the various elementary schools and now formed cliques within her class.

Finally a letter arrived from Nairobi. But Mother seemed displeased as she read it aloud at lunch and translated it.

"They say that we should get there first. Then they will decide and make the rest of the arrangements."

"They evidently do not realize what such a trip represents for us," Father grumbled too. "Imagine our going through with all this, and then they say April, April?"

"I don't believe that." Mother was forceful again.

"The African way is probably to calmly wait for events to happen. We Germans always want to organize everything thoroughly and in timely fashion."

"Anyway, even if they leave us in the lurch," Jochen said realistically, "we will have experienced Africa and the sun."

"But it would be such a terrible shame if we couldn't meet Alice!" Mareike was almost in tears.

"It will all work out. Not to worry," Mother concluded the discussion. "Heinz, check with the travel agency tomorrow about an inexpensive flight to Kenya."

In school the next morning, Mareike was not paying attention and could only repeat to herself: I hope it works out, I hope it works out. Naturally it had to be a morning when the teachers called on her several times, and she got bad marks.

When Mareike got home she had to unburden herself to Lolli first, since her parents weren't there yet.

"Cat, you are lucky you don't have to go to school," she whispered, and Lolli rubbed his head consolingly against her cheek. "Do you think things will work out with our visit to Alice?"

Lolli had no comment, but his large yellow eyes looked as though he himself were a big lonely lion in the grasslands of Kenya.

Finally her parents came home, together. Mother was restless and joined her husband at the travel agency. It was typical of her to want to organize everything herself, and she sometimes got on her family's nerves that way. But today Mareike was grateful that things were getting underway, and she looked at her mother with anticipation.

"Well, honey," Mother said and smiled, "what are we going to wear in the hot sun?"

"Does that mean that everything is OK?" Mareike asked, not yet daring to be happy.

"Well, we'll see," Father replied with caution. "In any case, we did book a flight to Mombasa for July, right at the start of summer vacation."

"Hooray," Mareike yelled, and she swung the

fat tomcat around so fast he suddenly looked like a poor sausage rather than like the king of the desert. "We're going to Africa!"

Jochen heard her shout from the front door, and he started to dance and shout, too. No longer did he look like the cool dancing class student.

"Easy, easy," Father warned them. "We'll fly to Mombasa, that's set. But how we get from there to Kitui remains to be seen."

"Why don't we take the train?" asked Mareike, who could not imagine that they couldn't reach any place in an inhabited land.

"The train only goes to Nairobi, and there are still many, many kilometers from there to Kitui."

"What about a rental car?" Mareike asked matter-of-factly.

"Who is going to drive in this unfamiliar area? Without regular roads or road signs, how are we going to find a tiny Akamba village?"

"Once we're in Kenya, we'll find a way to get to Alice." Mother concluded.

For the time being there was no further discussion about this, since nothing could be done anyway. Jochen was practically no longer thinking of the planned trip and the problems it created. He was all fire and flame over the instruction in the dancing school, and his "flame" there was a pretty dark-haired girl. He danced with her almost every Friday and it was clear that he would be taking Lisa—that was her name—to the graduation ball.

In March, just before Easter, another report arrived from Nairobi about Alice and her well-being. A school transcript was included, according to which Alice was No. 17 among the 56 students in her class.

"That's a sort of ranking, like in tennis," explained Mother. "Grades and marks are evaluated and listed from number one to the last one. We used to have that in Germany, too; you were even seated in the classroom according to your ranking."

"I'm glad we no longer have that here and now," said Jochen, who liked to decide whom he would sit next to and who had not had grades high enough to rank among the first ten.

Mareike preferred to sit in the back anyway, from where she could have a good overview of the class and didn't have to fear some dummy pinching her in the back or pulling her braid.

"In any case, this is a clear sign of life from Alice," Mother said. She debated for the nth time whether she should write to Alice about the trip and their intention of visiting her. But Mareike tried to talk her out of it again today.

"Just imagine if something goes wrong, one of us gets sick, or ..." Secretly she was thinking: or we don't find her, but she did not want to say that out loud. "She would be so dreadfully disappointed."

"Mareike is right," Jochen agreed, "don't write anything about the trip, just general blah-blah."

"And my learned son will write the second part of the letter in his fluent English," Mother decreed.

"And I will paint another portrait of Lolli and write under it, 'This is our cat,'" Mareike added.

So it was done, and the letter was finished in three days. It would certainly take ten days to reach Nairobi, and quite a bit of time would pass before it got to Kitui with a foodstuff shipment or such.

Mother secretly enclosed a brief note in the envelope, addressed to the "Ladies and Gentlemen" of the Organization, asking for their assistance for their trip to Kitui. She wrote in English, as she had done for the letters.

Some godparents of children in Africa, who did not speak that language, would simply write in German, and the Organization would translate. Naturally such letters took even longer.

Easter vacation arrived, as well as Jochen's dancing school graduation ball. His parents were just as excited about attending the ball as he was. It was the custom for the parents to participate in the festivity. The sons would then dance a waltz with their mothers, and the daughters with their fathers.

For Easter, they were again invited by their grandparents, and like every other year, they hunted for eggs and candy in the garden. They really did not want about their travel plans and about Alice, but it was Grandma who raised the subject.

"What are you going to do with your cat while you are away?" she asked.

They all looked at her with surprise.

"Well, I admit that the idea and the destination seem crazy to me," said Grandma, "but if it's got to be, at least the cat should not be a victim."

Mother looked gratefully at Grandma. "Would you really do that?"

"Well, then, I'll have at least one of you as a remembrance, just in case you don't come back from Africa," she said, and they all laughed.

Grandma sometimes had a funny sense of humor, and she was wise, too. She had understood long ago that her son Heinz and his energetic wife Vera knew what they wanted, and she did not want to have arguments and disagreements in the family.

*   *   *

After Easter, they really started to look forward to the trip and to accept it as a reality. One Saturday, Mareike burst out in school about it.

They were learning geography again with Miss Ruttlewski, who now called herself Ruttlewski-Flocke, because she got married during Easter vacation and wanted to have her husband's name as well. The name was very long, and the children found it difficult to address her. But clever old Jörgen said, "That's fine, call her by her name as often as you can. It will make the hour pass faster."

That made sense to them, and although in private, during recess, they called her "Flocke," in class they would always insistently use the tongue-twister Mrs. Ruttlewski-Flocke.

One Saturday morning, "Flocke" announced she wanted to tell them about human misery in the Third World. They were only fifth-graders and actually this was part of the seventh-grade curriculum, but in light of recent reports in the media—by which she meant newspapers and TV—even ten-year-olds should be told about the problems of this world, which were everyone's concern, after all. If they continued to eat nothing but hamburgers—i.e., ground beef—more and more tropical forests would be cut down to create cow pastures. And that has consequences for the whole world, but especially for these poor countries themselves. Thus, floods and dry spells are growing. And if they wanted to eat strawberries and beans from Africa, even in winter, this would affect the population there.

"We are going to Africa," Mareike blurted out. She actually hadn't meant to say it out loud, but the thought went through her head like a flash, and out it came.

"Is that a fact?" Mrs. Ruttlewski-Flocke asked with surprise, and they all turned to look at Mareike.

"Yes, really, this year in July," she started to say, but Susan in the first row interrupted, "I've been to Africa already."

"Where in Africa?" they all asked Susan, who had more friends than Mareike because she was louder and more amusing.

"In Tunisia, Christmas before last," she answered. "And we saw real belly dancing."

"Well, in North Africa conditions are different than in Black Africa," Flocke said calmly, "and I really wanted to tell you about arid regions and dry spells in Central Africa, but go ahead, you report first."

Susan described the hotel on the Mediterranean, the palms and the camels, and a dance evening on Christmas Eve, and the children listened with fascination.

"And you could actually swim in the sea when we had snow here?" one of them asked wistfully.

"Yes, every day," Susan assured him, and failed to mention that she had been so afraid of any jellyfish or Portuguese man-of-war that she had chosen to swim in the hotel's pool.

No, there weren't many Negroes, she responded to another question, only Arabs, brown people with aquiline noses.

"People don't say 'Negroes' anymore," Mareike interrupted timidly. "They say 'Blacks.'"

"Right, Mareike." Flocke smiled at her. "Now you tell us where you are going to travel."

"We are going to Kenya to visit Alice," Mareike said, and floundered a little at first. But then, when she thought of the snapshot and the long reports from the Organization, her words started to flow freely.

The class had turned away from Susan and was now listening to Mareike. Unfortunately the bell rang—much too early, they all thought, and that was unusual because normally everyone waited for the bell.

"Next class I will show you a film about Kenya," Flocke promised. "Homework: summarize what you have learned today."

As usual there was grumbling, although retelling was a simply assignment, but complaining is just part of school life.

Before homeroom, Susan came up to Mareike. "I think that's keen," she said. "You must tell me more."

Mareike had actually been afraid that Susan had resented her interruption. After all, she hadn't been able to finish her story. But Susan appeared to be a good sport; she was not sore at all, only curious.

They walked together to the subway station, and they talked and talked, until they had to take different trains.

The weekend was pleasant and tranquil as usual, and the first days of the week went by for Mareike like in a dream. She was waiting for Wednesday and the Flocke movie.

Finally the day came. Jörg and Andreas brought the film projector from the equipment room; they had accepted to be assistants for this class. Mareike didn't yet have a school job and would not have liked to be responsible for such equipment. What if you dropped any of it? But today she watched with interest how the two boys set up the folding table and placed the projector on it.

"In other schools they have had video machines

for a long time," said one of them. "Such super-8 film is really prehistorical."

But when Flocke entered the classroom with the thick film reel, they were all quiet and excited.

"I am not showing you a movie about beaches and palms and natives," she said. "You have seen those in a lot of TV programs, even in commercials ..."

"The 'Sun Glow' commercials are like that," Ann exclaimed flippantly, and Flocke laughed.

"You see, you have known for a long time how things look in Africa. But this film shows rare scenes from the life of nomads in Kenya and Tanzania. Does anyone know what nomads are?"

No one answered at first, but then Oliver, who read a lot of Karl May, said, "They're tribes that wander with their herds."

"Very good, Oliver," Flocke praised him. "One could hardly express it any better. Now, the largest nomadic tribe in this area are the Masai," she explained as she threaded in the film.

"They wander endlessly through the land with their cattle herds. I hope this film will teach you the consequences of this way of life."

"When do they go to school?" asked Andreas, who would have preferred a carefree existence.

"Almost not at all," replied the teacher, "much to the chagrin of the Kenyan government, which is very progressive. The government does a lot to make this people sedentary and to provide some education for them. But they are hard to tie down."

"I can understand that," mumbled Andreas. "Long live freedom."

"Let's first look at how these Masai live, before we discuss the advantages and disadvantages," Flocke decided. "Lights out, please."

Kenya is twice as large as the Federal Republic of Germany and has a population of 22 million, i.e., not even half that of our own country. One might therefore assume: That's enough for everybody, enough space and food. And we all know the pictures: white beaches, palms, immense animal reservations . . .

But the first impression is deceptive. Only one fourth of the country can be used for agriculture, and that is often coffee, tea, and sisal plantations; wealth for a small number of people.

The mass of the population is poor and dreams of owning its own piece of land, a "Shamba." Much fertile land has been stripped by the cattle herds of the nomads; elsewhere forest trees are cut down or burned because firewood and charcoal are needed. Fields are planted on the scorched earth, but they don't bear fruit for long.

Even if all this could be changed—but who can and will change millenary customs?—there

The movie began with a vast panorama. A white plain surrounded in the distance by hills. Short, yellowish grass in which grew isolated trees with umbrella-shaped tops. Animals then approached from far away that turned out to be a herd of cattle. But the cattle were small and brownish and hardly looked like German cows. Two tall people followed them; they carried long sticks and looked with large eyes calmly into the camera.

"But these aren't Negroes at all," cried someone in the classroom.

is always one factor that cannot be changed: the climate. How often has our Alice written to us: "We have planted beans, but they have dried out because the rains have not come." So, even this vast land must import foodstuff to feed its people. And their number grows steadily. The Kenyans love children, and need them to work in the home and in the field and to care for the old ones. Each year, the population grows by 4 percent, and more children create more problems. In the slums of Nairobi, the capital, you can see many unemployed youngsters hanging around. They are attracted to the city, by its amusements, by the white tourists who all seem to be so rich. Tourism, which brings much money into the country, thus also has a dark side. It creates false standards yardsticks, causes envy and greed. In spite of all that, Kenya is considered a model African country. It won independence twenty-six years ago ("Uhuru" was the battle cry) and is governed today by President Daniel Arap Moi.

"That's a good observation," commented Mrs. Ruttlewski-Flocke. "Although these Masai are dark-skinned, they are not really Blacks. They are supposed to have come from North Africa long ago, from the Nile. That's why they are called a Nilotic people."

The movie then showed a whole group of these beautiful tall people who were wrapped in simple cloths but wore bunches of colorful hoops around their necks.

"But they're red-haired," called out Arne from the back of the class.

"They are dyed by the red dust of the steppe," Flocke explained. "You will soon see the dance of the warriors, who carry even more colorful ornaments and daub themselves with paint."

The children liked the next scene, the rhythmic dancing, the drums, the fierce movements of the dancers, the expressive faces ...

"That's how I've always imagined Indian war dances," said one boy, and Flocke didn't contradict him.

The dance episode was followed by village scenes. Round huts were arranged in a circle surrounded by thorny branches.

"That is a kraal," Flocke commented. "The Masai build these out of clay and branches for a certain length of time. When the whole area has been grazed out by their cattle, they move on, burning the huts behind them."

"How convenient," remarked one girl. "They don't have to tidy up or clean their houses."

"But a piece of land has been destroyed," said Flocke, "especially by the hooves of the cattle."

"Do the Masai still go hunting?" Mareike asked, for she had noticed that the men carried spears.

"Sure," said the teacher, "but mainly, they live from the milk and blood of their cattle."

"Blood?" shrieked some of the children, and Flocke laughed because they sounded so horrified.

"They don't kill the animals for the blood. They tap it from their necks and seal the cut with a plug."

"Yuk!" many of the children cried, and Mareike also shuddered.

"That's cruelty to animals," Jörg said with outrage, and Mareike was surprised because she had not given him credit for such sensitivity. Jörg always swaggered like a big, cool hombre.

"That may be," answered Flocke, "but the Masai would certainly consider as cruel many of the things we do to animals, like locking them up in narrow cages, for example."

The movie and the class were over much too fast, and Flocke promised to answer the rest of the questions during geography class on Saturday.

"If I can," she said honestly. "I have never been in that country either. When Mareike comes back from her travels, she'll be able to tell you more about it."

Mareike was proud about this prospect, but also a little scared. The letters from Alice and the welfare organization said nothing about wild nomadic tribes; they made it sound quite different there, almost normal. Alice went to school, she helped with work in the garden and in the fields, and she needed a new dress at the start of each school year. Blood and milk had not been mentioned in the reports about her life, only the planting of beans and how bad things were when they dried up for lack of water. But Alice belonged to the Akamba tribe, who lived in permanent villages. The differences between tribes in Kenya were probably just as great as the differences between Bavarians and Berliners in Germany. Different Germans also had trouble understanding each other when they spoke their dialects, and up at the North Sea they only knew Lederhosen or Schuhplattler through movies or visits to Southern Germany.

Would they really meet Alice? Mother hadn't

received another letter from the Organization's office in Nairobi yet. Only the last note in which they said, Sure, just come on over, and then we'll see.

But Mother was not worried, or at least she didn't act worried.

"Just remember that reports are due soon and that you should continue to study hard," she said.

"She is right," Jochen sighed. "Your most recent class participation often decides your grade."

Instead of cramming, he would have preferred to go to the outdoor swimming pool more often. Ever since the dancing lessons he got together with his classmates at the swimming pool and also with the girl who had been his dancing partner. He had already acquired quite a tan in the summer sun.

"You'll soon look like an African yourself," Mareike said enviously. She was still pale because she spent so much time indoors. She was studying for school because she wanted to end her first year in secondary school with good grades, and also she had long telephone talks with Susan, chatting about anything and everything in their lives.

Lolli created the problem that almost ruined the whole trip. To be precise, not Lolli but Grandma. Two weeks before the vacation she got sick. Nothing serious, and she didn't have to go to the hospital, but the gastrointestinal infection made her so weak that Grandpa declared loudly, "You cannot impose the cat on her now." How were they going to find a good cat person and get him the required shots on such short notice?

But four days before they left, Grandpa called and said, "All right, you can come and bring the cat.

Your grandmother is up and about, and she says she's feeling young and strong again."

"I hope she isn't just saying that to reassure Grandpa and to relieve us of the worry," Mother wondered. "Heinz, what do you think?"

Heinz knew his mother best and said, "Don't worry. If that's what she wants, she'll manage. We'll drive there tomorrow and deliver the cat."

That's what they did, and Mother also brought six glasses of her best gooseberry jam as a little token of appreciation.

"We have to bring back something neat from our trip," said Jochen. "Maybe a Masai spear for Grandpa."

"Or some necklace of colorful beads for Grandma," Mareike added, and they all giggled in the car, picturing Grandma's lined face and her neat, curly white hairdo with the native ornament.

They were still chuckling when they arrived at their grandparents' home, and Grandpa asked amiably: "Well, are you looking forward to this vacation?"

"You bet," Jochen and Mareike cried out together in their excitement.

"But first we are going to get our report cards," Jochen groaned. He didn't have too good a feeling because he had loafed a bit that semester. He had preferred dancing lessons and swimming to learning vocabulary and historic dates. He was sure he'd be promoted to the next grade, of course, but he was afraid there might be one or two poor marks.

Their good mood dropped when they had to leave Lolli behind. He was offended, anyway, because they had locked him in the cat basket for the ride.

"It's safer that way," said Father, who was

driving. "Otherwise he might jump on my shoulder like last time and make me let go of the steering wheel."

"Bye-bye, old pussycat," Mareike whispered, and her eyes filled with tears. "Don't forget us. I'll bring you something nice from Africa."

"Maybe a coconut to play with," Jochen proposed, and his voice was also weak and unsteady.

The next day the report cards arrived and, after examining them at length, their parents said at lunch, "Not bad, after all. You both earned the trip."

"Would I have had to stay here, if I hadn't been promoted?" Jochen asked with fear and trepidation. Father replied, "Of course. What did you think? You would have had to cram during the whole vacation! But we won't even think about such a possibility. Anyone who studies regularly never has to repeat a grade."

"Well, I don't know," Jochen started to say, but he paused when Mareike kicked him in the shins under the table. Father was almost grinning despite his severe statement, so why ask for more?

They had a great surprise when they went to bid farewell to their neighbors.

"But where is the cat?" asked Mrs. Hördelmann, the bird lover. "You could easily have left him with me. He's been eating his second breakfast here pretty often."

Well, what do you know? Lolli had managed to charm this lady, too, with his long whiskers. And now they knew why he was getting fatter and fatter. On the sly he was eating all the forbidden goodies he loved.

But it's a good feeling when you live in peace with the neighbors and there is no tension.

The next morning they were finally, finally on their way. Mareike barely slept all night, and woke up repeatedly to check the time on the clock in the belly of the plastic mouse whose eyes shone in the dark. The hands of the clock were illuminated and she could observe how they showed four o'clock, six o'clock, seven o'clock, and then she just had to get out of bed.

Mother looked surprised when Mareike came to the kitchen, and she stroked her daughter's rumpled hair.

"Well, well. The first day of vacation and you get up so early? But I understand, I'm so excited myself. I worry all the time whether I've packed everything."

"Oh, we won't need all that much down there in the hot weather," said Mareike, for luggage was not important to her.

"You're right, of course, but you know how many things I've packed for Alice and the other children, and I wonder what the customs people will say when they find two suitcases full of baby clothes and toys."

Mother had been rummaging in the basement and the attic, and often repeated how sorry she was that she had given away so many things from the children's early childhood. "I'm sure they could have made good use of them in Migwani."

"The Red Cross certainly passed your things on to people who needed them and who were happy to receive them," Father had commiserated. "There is need everywhere."

"Of course, of course," Mother mumbled, and she asked Mareike once again, "What has gotten too small for you recently?"—so she could pack it for Alice.

Mareike took the opportunity to drag up all the ruffled blouses that she couldn't stand anyway. She was happy to get rid of them, and even felt a little noble for having given them to needy children. Her new friend Susan would certainly not have done it with such a light heart, because she was very attached to her clothes and always needed more, so she could wear something different every day.

But now, on the morning of departure day, the suitcases were locked and Father said emphatically, "They'll now stay locked!" He finally came down for breakfast at eight o'clock.

"The best thing is for me to carry them down to the car right away, so we can spend the last hour here quietly without rushing."

It did not turn out to be all that quiet, for at the last minute they couldn't agree who had packed the malaria tablets.

"None of us," Jochen finally said. "They're still in the bathroom upstairs because we were supposed to take some last night."

He was right: for weeks they had been taking these tablets as a prophylactic to prevent catching this dangerous disease in Africa. It can be transmitted by a mosquito bite and gives you fever and shaking chills, and is very difficult to recover from.

"Well then, run upstairs and get them," exclaimed Mother, who was getting more and more nervous.

"Easy, honey," Father said soothingly. "We have an hour's drive to the airport, and then we have another two hours before the plane takes off."

"I wish we were already sitting in the plane,"

Mother sighed, and the kids agreed with her, not from exhaustion but from curiosity and excitement.

The moment finally arrived. They sat next to each other in the non-smoking section, Jochen by the window, then Mareike, Mother, and Father, who could stretch his long legs in the aisle. The loudspeakers were playing soft music, and pretty young stewardesses were circulating, smiling agreeably and helping with the stowing of bags and fastening of seat belts. Then the engines began to whine.

The sound grew until Mareike's ears were throbbing and she pressed her hands to her head and closed her eyes. When she opened them again they were already soaring above the ground and the houses became smaller by the second.

Jochen pressed his nose against the small round window and hummed with excitement. Mareike squinted past him and was afraid she was going to be sick, but to her relief she felt at peace and didn't need to throw up, as she sometimes did on amusement park rides.

Mother was very silent and looked solemnly forward. They didn't know whether she was holding her breath from fear or was really so relaxed. But then Father took her hand, held it tight and said, "You see, everything's in order. In eight hours we'll be in Africa."

The hours literally seemed to fly by. First they had a delicious meal with which they could drink anything they wanted. Then they saw the movie "A Clean Sweep" that Jochen watched excitedly.

Passengers who wanted to rest were given blankets and could put headphones over their ears. Mareike finally did just that, and the soft music lulled her to sleep. She dreamed that Lollipop was under a palm tree, playing with a coconut.

When she woke up, she thought she was in heaven. Not the one the airplane was actually floating through, but in the pretty heaven that picture books show. Outside there were pink cotton clouds, and Mareike would not have been surprised to see a little angel with golden wings flutter by, like the ones you find on Christmas cakes. But she was careful not to tell Jochen about her fantasies.

"What will we get to eat in Africa?" Mother wondered out loud.

"If we have to, we can subsist on bananas. They're easy to digest and contain everything you need to live on," Jochen announced with his eye for the practical solution.

"Oh, yes," said Mareike, who did not care much for meat, potatoes, and gravy. She preferred fruit and vegetables. Unfortunately sweets as well.

There was another announcement over the loudspeakers in English, and Mother listened attentively.

"We're landing in Mombasa in twenty minutes," she translated. "Local time is 7:40 p.m., air temperature is twenty-nine degrees centigrade."

The stewardesses came around with baskets of damp, hot, steaming towels. Mareike asked incredulously, "Do we have to wash our hands so we'll not bring in pollution?"

"Of course not," explained Father, who had already flown abroad many times, "on business" as he called it. "You place them on your face and feel refreshed and ready to go after the long flight."

"I do feel ready to go," Mareike objected, "and I don't want that hot rag."

She took one carefully, just the same, and let

out a squeak when she felt the heat on her nose. But then the towel and her face cooled down, and she really felt freshly bathed.

The plane finally touched down very softly on the landing strip, and the passengers applauded. Then everybody hurried to get the bags down from the overhead compartments and up from under the seats, and Father reminded them again, "Don't rush, the travel agency bus is waiting for us and will take us to the hotel. Just let the others get out first."

They left the plane and stepped into a wall of hot, humid air that made their clothes stick to their bodies.

"Wow, what heat," Jochen groaned, and Mother pushed strands of hair from her forehead. The only thing they could see of the airport was the brightly lit arrival hall. Everything else was already in total darkness.

"That's the way it is in the tropics," Father informed them. "There is no long twilight like in our regions. Nightfall comes suddenly. And the light comes just as fast in the morning. You'll see."

Their passports were checked by a friendly black woman who greeted every passenger with "Jambo."

"Jambo" means "Good day," they already knew, and they responded the same way whenever they heard "Jambo," with broad friendly smiles and sparkling white teeth—at the coffee counter, at the passage to the waiting room, and by the travel agency representative whom they easily recognized by the large sign he was holding up.

Jambo, Africa, welcome to Kenya!

They were all loaded with their suitcases, carry-on-bags, overnight bags, and umbrellas into a travel agency bus and were dropped at the various hotels where they had reservations.

They drove through the city of Mombasa, but it was dark and the streetlights were dim. Only in front of the restaurants and hotels were the lights bright, and Mareike tried to get a better look at the groups of Blacks assembled there. But that was difficult because the bus windows were tinted glass, and dark faces are difficult to see in the dark. A few times she felt a little fearful when the exotic people in their colorful garb looked at their bus, but then some dark young man in jeans would show up and laugh, and everything would seem normal and familiar again.

Their hotel was the last one on the route.

"It's farthest away from town and the cheapest," said Father, and Jochen made a face since they had stopped at some really great hotels.

"That has its advantages, too," Mother said. "Don't forget, we have a small bungalow just for ourselves."

"Let's hope it isn't a hut with a thatched roof," mumbled Jochen. He was tired and sounded tense.

Mareike didn't say anything. She agreed to everything. After all, she was really and truly in Africa, a continent she had known only from movies and books and where Alice, her black sister, lived.

As they drove onto the hotel grounds of the Giriama Apartments, she spotted two tall black men with nightsticks at the gate. The bus stopped in front of the faintly lit entrance to the central building, and the two black men slowly came up to the bus in which the travel guide and the last remaining passengers were sitting.

"For heaven's sake, Heinz," Mother whispered. "Let's not get out. They look frightening."

But Johnny, the German-speaking representative of the travel agency, heard her although he was sitting in front next to the driver and they were at the back of the bus.

"Don't worry, Madame," he said. "These are just the guards of this place. They make sure that there is no one running around here at night who doesn't belong here."

"Well, that sounds very reassuring," said Father. He rose to get the bags out of the luggage racks. Mother and the children followed him and, after a last handshake with Johnny, they found themselves at last at the reception desk. Surrounded by all their luggage, they faced a young Black in a snow-white shirt who spoke only English. He said "Jambo" several times, like all the people at the airport, picked up Mother's suitcase, and gestured to them to follow him. He would show them the little house that would be their home for the next two weeks.

Past the two dark guards with their big clubs, they walked paved paths among fragrant bushes and tall trees that they couldn't identify in the jet-black night. A little light shone out of the small boxy house.

"You see, Jochen," Mother remarked. "Not a native hut."

Music and voices could be heard from a larger building nearby. The bellboy said something to them, and Father declared, "That's where the restaurant is where we can eat and drink."

"And dance in the evening," Jochen said, half-asking.

"That too, no doubt," replied Father. "but not tonight please, I'm bushed."

"What a shame," Mother said innocently. "I was looking forward to a shindig under the palms."

"Where's the beach?" asked Mareike. They had booked in a beach hotel, directly on the shore of the Indian Ocean. But she couldn't hear the kind of ocean sounds she knew from a few weeks of vacation on the North Sea.

"We'll look for it tomorrow," Mother promised, and then yelped in fear when something moved in front of her feet and disappeared in the bushes.

"Snake or lizard," declared the bellboy. "Not dangerous. But better wear shoes."

"My God, that's all I need," sighed Mother, who loved animals but also got scared when a spider or bug ran through the house.

They were all a little uptight now, because they were tired and everything seemed so dark and foreign around them. When the bellboy finally opened the door to their little house and turned on a rather dim light, their mood wasn't lifted. They found themselves in a simple living room in which a kitchen corner had been built at one end. Connected to it were two bedrooms with two couches each.

"I wonder whether they wash the covers from time to time?" Mother asked and looked with suspicion at the pink-red objects.

"Don't be so picky, honey," replied her husband. "You're not in your well-kept single-family home here, but in Africa, and for our money we couldn't afford anything better for the four of us."

"It's all right," she said, and squeezed his arm. Then she gave a tip to the bellboy waiting at the door.

"Ten Kenya shillings, Was that enough?" she

asked, and Father said, "Divide by six—that makes one mark fifty. Yes, I think that's fine."

Then they were by themselves. The children turned on all the lights and examined the little house.

"This leads to the terrace," said Jochen. "Here through the sliding door."

"You had better keep it closed for the time being," said Father, "to keep bugs and animals out. We'll eat our breakfast out there tomorrow morning."

"I'm not going to do any cooking here," Mother said with finality. "The kitchen is swarming with ants."

They all rushed in to see them: the little brown insects crawled out of the washbasin's overflow and ran busily to and fro, over the counter, up the cupboard, onto the floor and back again.

"I even know why they're here," said Mareike. "There are some sugar cubes here. They love that."

"Out with them," ordered Mother. "We'll drink tea without sugar tomorrow. Better than with ants."

She picked up the little bowl and looked around, searching.

"In front of the door, there's a trash can, I think," said Jochen who always quickly noticed everything important. "Let me have it. I'll pour the sugar there."

"Can't you take the ants, too?" Mother pleaded. One could see that she wasn't feeling pleased.

"By tomorrow they'll disappear, when there is nothing left for them to eat," Father assured her.

"Oh, in this clammy kitchen there's still enough to attract the creatures," Mother said in the same pleading voice that she had never used before. "I'll have to clean up thoroughly tomorrow."

"You are not going to do housework here,"

Father decided. "Now go sit in the easy chair over there and take a sip of the cognac I bought in the airplane, and the kids and I will unpack."

Mother obeyed and sat there like a symbol of misery. The children made every effort to distribute the things logically in the two rooms.

"It's not really great that we have to sleep together," Jochen grumbled, but Father had a solution here, too. "Occasionally we can switch, then we two men can sleep in one room, and the two women in the other.

"Help," Mother cried from the living room. "Help, don't leave me all alone."

They stormed into the room and found her standing on the armchair, staring at the floor with big eyes, "Something ran through here again."

"Yuk!" Mareike was also getting a creepy feeling.

"A lizard," Jochen cried triumphantly, holding up the small, blue-green animal anxiously swishing its tail.

"Lizards in the living room! Heinz, even with all my love for animals and for Africa, I've had it!"

"I read in our guidebook that these animals are considered useful and are raised specially because they catch mosquitoes and other insects," Father reassured her. "You should be grateful to them for protecting us against pests."

Mareike, who had been bitten several times on the way through the building and garden of the hotel, found this thought comforting and said to Mother, "So, you see, and they're such cute animals."

"Maybe," Mother groaned, and stepped down from the chair, "but please get this one out of the house. I'm going to bed now and will shut my eyes."

"Have another cognac," her husband recommended. "We are going to clean up here and we'll go to bed early, too—right, kids?"

"Gee," whined Jochen who would haved liked to explore outside. "How are we going to sleep in this heat?"

"Turn on the air conditioning," said Father, pointing at the large boxes in the wall. Jochen acted according. This resulted in a mighty roar and whirling.

"That's like at the airport," Mareike yelled. "How can we sleep with that noise?"

"You're right, dear," Mother cried from her couch. "We'd rather sweat than go out of our minds. We'll just cover up with the thin sheets," and she hurled the pink-red nylon blanket into the corner.

Jochen turned the ventilator off, and they fell into bed after a quick wash. "Even the cold shower is warm here," Mareike announced from behind the shower curtain.

Mareike couldn't fall asleep for a long while. Her thin nightgown was sticking to her body and even the sheet felt too warm. She heard rustling and humming around her as though thousands of little creatures were at work. Finally, she wrapped herself in the sheet up to her nose, for the idea that a lizard might run over her face during the night didn't appeal to her.

When she woke up in the morning, sunlight was shining brightly through the thin white window curtains, and she knew right away where she was. She was in Africa, Kenya, Mombasa, the Giriama Hotel grounds—hunger, thirst, heat. And a strange odor, half sweet, half moldy.

Jochen's bed was already empty, and she heard the clinking of cups in the living room. She ran in there and found her parents drinking tea. Mother was already wearing a colorful beach dress, and Father had on shorts and a bright red T-shirt they had never seem him wear at home.

"Good morning, dearie," Mother said. "Did you sleep well?"

"Yes, like a log," Mareike replied, and said nothing about the clammy bed and her fear of crawling creatures. "Where is Jochen?"

"He's already looking around outside," Father pointed at the wide-open terrace door.

Mareike went outside as she was, barefoot and in her short nightgown, and took a deep breath. There were flowering bushes everywhere, with enormous red and yellow blossoms, and tall palm trees overhead, and the sky was as blue as on a postcard.

"Boy, is this keen," she called, and Mother joined her, smiling.

"You see," she said, and all the apprehension of the night before was gone, "now come drink a cup of tea, put on something light, and we'll all go to the restaurant to have a real breakfast."

"Oh, yes." Mareike beamed, ran into the bathroom, a little water, a little toothpaste, a band around her hair and into shorts and a blouse.

"Funny, during the school year we never get dressed as fast as on vacation," Father laughed. "For school I always have to wait and lean on the horn..."

Mareike would have had plenty to say on that subject: the anticipation of something beautiful as compared with the dreariness of going to school and attending classes, but Father already knew all that. After all, he didn't go to his office in a bright red shirt either.

"Put on your sandals," Mother said, and Mareike obeyed, although the shimmering lizards darting across her path on the way through the grounds no longer seemed frightening or repellent to her at all. Mother felt the same way and looked around with delight.

They found Jochen in front of the house, motionless on a rock, pointing his camera.

"Hush," he hissed. "That's one I've got to photograph," and he pointed with his head to a bright blue lizard that was certainly as long as Mareike's arm, hand to elbow.

"You'll have plenty of time for that," Father laughed. "Now come with us for breakfast before we visit the beach."

But even on their walk through the garden, they could already see the sea, glistening behind a row of tall palm trees all the way to the horizon.

"The Indian Ocean," Mother said with some excitement. "Normally we know it only from fairy tales and old adventure stories."

"Children, now we're living our own adventure," Father beamed, "far away from Germany, from my office and my files."

"And from school," Jochen added. But Mareike said, "Well, these seem to be German schoolchildren, too," for a group was coming toward them wearing T-shirts and sporting words and phrases that were popular in her school. As they ran past them, they could hear them speak German with an unmistakable Rhinelander accent.

"Oh, God," Jochen groaned. "Let's pretend to be English."

"That may work for you and Mother," Father

said, "but Mareike and I could only pretend to be both English and deaf mutes."

"Or slightly deranged," Mareike proposed.

"Please don't," Mother said. "Act natural and choose the children you want to play with."

"Blacks!" Mareike cried, but there were no Black children here. Black gardeners were working on the paths, raking and picking up faded blossoms. In the restaurants the waiters were Blacks, but all the guests were white: German, English, Italian; a mixture of languages and clothes. Some wore correct trousers and shirts, others were in swimsuits.

The restaurant was open on one side, and they could see all the way to the ocean, and run down there, which some of them did right after breakfast.

A bellboy in a snow-white coat and black trousers led them to their table with a smile.

"Tea or coffee," he asked, and that much English they could all understand. He then gave them a large menu.

"You can have fried eggs, scrambled eggs, eggs and bacon, eggs and ham, soft-boiled eggs..."

"Anything else?" Jochen interrupted his mother. He didn't like eggs.

"Grilled sausage, grilled bacon, grilled fish, toast, orange jam, corn flakes," she read on, and Mareike cried, "Oh, please, corn flakes with lots of milk and sugar for me. And hot chocolate."

"Roasted ants are also supposed to be good," said Jochen, and Mareike nearly choked on her chocolate. She eyed her corn flakes suspiciously to see whether any ants were crawling through them, but everything was okay.

After this ample breakfast they set out on an exploration expedition.

*　*　*

The hotel garden went all the way down to the beach and ended at a white-daubed gate that was wide open. Behind it there was nothing but sand, just as white as the gate, but glistening and glittering so they could barely look at it. Wide and endless.

Then there came a strip of land that looked dark and damp, on which were lying strangely shaped branches, looking like old bones, and then came the ocean, the water, the sea. White and green and blue, with golden highlights and white crests—it was so vast, so beautiful and overpowering that even the most vivid fantasy could not have imagined it. Mareike wanted to rush forward, through the sand, into the water, but then she saw her parents who had stopped in their tracks gazing into the endless expanse.

"The Indian Ocean," Mother said softly. "Mombasa—Malindi—Zanzibar ..." Her voice sounded as though she were about to recite a fairy tale, as she used to do by the children's bed every evening.

"It's like a fairy tale," she said, "Heinz, to think that we're allowed to experience this."

"You can thank your dear Aunt Hedwig," her husband replied. "Without her we'd now be standing under the gray clouds of the North Sea."

Jochen was getting restless. "Why did you mention these particular names?" he asked. "The name Zanzibar is familiar from somewhere."

"Doubtless from old seafarer's tales," Mother answered, and she slowly walked on through the white sand. "For more than a thousand years, this shore was a trading center for gold, ivory, spices, slaves ..."

"Slaves?" Mareike asked, horrified.

"Yes. In fact this was a transfer point for the slave trade, which was only forbidden about a hundred years ago."

"Good heavens!" Mareike was shocked and now looked at the shoreline with different eyes. "Thank goodness this doesn't exist anymore and Alice doesn't have to become a slave."

"Then we would have bought her freedom," said Jochen, who always had a solution for everything.

"I don't know whether it would have been that easy," Father laughed. "But let's go, the sun is cooking my brain."

"We must absolutely buy some sun hats," Mother said, "and wear our beach sandals."

Disapprovingly, she looked at Jochen who was the only barefoot one. As they continued to scamper on the sun-drenched sand, he jerked a foot up from time to time and yelled, "Ouch, is that hot!"

"There, you see," Mother said with an I-told-you-so look, "that's what you get for not listening to me."

"We could go swimming," suggested her smart big son. "I'm sure the water is cooler."

"But this seems to be low tide," Father said, looking at the wide, damp strip between the dry sand and the gently rippling water.

"Come on, let's see what we can find here. That was always exciting at the North Sea on the tidelands."

"Starfish," Mareike shouted. "dozens and dozens of living starfish."

She crouched down and examined the funny creatures in the damp sand, often hidden between green seaweed and porous rocks, with sometimes only three arms protruding. She did not find them nasty at all and would have touched them. But she imagined how much they would resent that: to be suddenly lifted out of a moist hiding place into the bright sun. No, she could do without that kind of a game.

Jochen was stalking along stiffly like a stork because he did not want to feel all those animals and sharp stones under his bare feet. Then a black man appeared out of nowhere.

"Shells, madame, fine shells?

They turned around, startled, to see a smiling face with widely spaced teeth. The man had large brown shells in his hands, and he showed them eagerly.

"Oh, they're beautiful," Mareike exclaimed, and picked one of the shells that had a pattern like a jungle cat. "Please, please, buy this one."

Their parents were also examining the beautiful objects from the sea. While they were holding a shell in their hands and wanted to haggle about the price in a mixture of German, English, and sign language, another man joined the group. He was white, wore rolled-up jeans, and addressed them in German.

"Be careful. It is strictly forbidden to take these things out of the country. Nature conservation, you know."

"But the man found them, the shells are dead anyway," Mother said as she turned the yellow-pink shell in her hand.

The white man shook his head and said, "Look out there toward the reef." He pointed with the hand at a string of low rocks in the water.

"That is exposed at low tide. The Blacks then go and detach the clams from the rocks and kill them. And they sell the pretty shells to tourists."

"That's awful." Mother was horrified and quickly returned the shell to the Black man, who had been listening half anxiously, half curiously, to the German conversation.

"That's right," said the nature friend, "and if each tourist were to take just one shell out of the country, the beach would be empty one day."

"But just one," persisted Mareike, who didn't want to let go of the beautiful thing.

"You would have the greatest problems at departure from the airport, believe me. If the officials find any protected nature products in your possession, shells, corals, ivory, furs, you will not be permitted to board the airplane."

"Really?" Father wondered. "It's a good thing you warned us. Imagine the bother. And I'm for obeying the law."

"My father is a lawyer," Mareike proudly informed the stranger.

He introduced himself, "Mertens, from Bremen."

"Gantenbein," Father said, "from Essen."

Meanwhile they had returned all the shells to the Black man who walked away with a knowing expression.

"He'll try it again with the next ones," Mr. Mertens predicted.

Together they walked along the beach for almost two hours. There was so much to see! To their left was the row of palms that formed the edge of the beach hotel gardens and opened up to snow-white buildings, some large and magnificent, others merely boxes like their own at the Giriama Apartments. To their right, the ocean rushed in in long calm waves and sometimes reached their feet, and burning above it all was the African midday sun.

Several other Blacks also offered them shells and pieces of coral, but the parents refused with a shake of their heads. At first, Mother had spoken in measured English about laws and nature conservation. The youths knew all that, of course, after all they were citizens of the country, but they smilingly submitted to Mother's fervent teaching, shrugged their shoulders, and sauntered on to try their luck with someone else. But when one of them offered a split coconut from which the milk could be sucked with straws, the family eagerly accepted. Everyone did that here; surely it wasn't forbidden, and the morning had made them thirsty.

"Tastes wonderful," said Jochen.

But Mother wanted to get back to the hotel.

"Maybe there is mail from Nairobi at the desk for me," she said hopefully. "I wrote to the Organization to tell them our arrival date and to ask that they let us know right away when and how we could visit Alice.   Besides, I'm exhausted," she concluded.

"Little wonder," Father said, "after the long flight, the hot night, and our walk in the sun—the best thing is we all take some rest after lunch. In bed or in the shade."

"Not me," Jochen objected. "I want to get back to the beach and go swimming. In the afternoon the high tide should be in."

"Well, I don't really know," Mother said skeptically, "whether this is a supervised beach with lifeguards and lifeboats."

"Look at the tall men carrying spears." Mareike pointed toward a group of palm trees. "Maybe they're the lifeguards. And when you go down, they might poke you with their spears and pull you out."

Jochen laughed and seemed to have no fear.

"I think they were there for decoration, or to sell their spears," Mother guessed. "Hey, could those be the famous Masai? They looked very different from the other Blacks, not so round and small."

Mareike remembered the film that Flocke had shown them in geography class.

"You're right, that's the way they must look. But they are supposed to live on the steppe with their cattle."

"A few of them must have discovered that you can milk tourists, too," Father said.

Even along the last few meters back to the hotel they were offered all sorts of things to buy. Mostly black carvings representing animals, human heads, and masks.

When they reached the hotel they went to their little cottage to freshen up. Mother ran off immediately to check for mail but she was back in no time.

"Still nothing!" She looked downcast.

Mareike asked doubtfully, "Are we really going to get to see Alice? Everything is so far away and foreign ..."

"You'll get your letter in a few days, I'm sure," Father consoled her. "We've gotten as far as Kenya. That is the most important for now."

But in the next three days, there still was no news. So they spent their time swimming, sunbathing, and beachcombing. Everything was so interesting that they barely remembered the little black girl who had actually been the reason for the trip. Only Mother went every morning to the office to ask for mail, but she no longer talked about her frustration.

Of the four, Jochen had the deepest tan. He was out at six o'clock in the morning, and he explored everything. If nightfall hadn't always come abruptly at six p.m., and the sun hadn't promptly risen at six a.m. like clockwork twelve hours later, he would barely have gotten any sleep. He already knew most of the people at the Giriama Apartments and even knew what that name stood for: a native tribe that lived here by the seashore. But he did not visit the discotheque, after trying it one evening. The open restaurant was rearranged a little bit after dinner, i.e. an area was cleared for dancing, colored light bulbs and a roaring stereo system were turned on—and that was it. Fat white men then met there with their black or white girlfriends and shuffled panting and sweating across the floor. And a few German and English teenagers hung around and were pushed aside like bothersome little children. After all, they didn't drink alcohol as the old ones did, by the liter, and so the barman didn't earn much from them. A coke cost only fifty pfennigs, at the exchange rate.

Jochen didn't like that atmosphere. He had just learned from pretty dancing teachers to glide elegantly over shining parquet, and he didn't feel like shoving and jostling among flabby fannies.

So they usually sat together in the evening, reading, listening to the radio which was built into the living room, and talking about their experience. One evening, in the bedroom, Jochen secretly showed his sister two shells. They were not large and had wonderfully pretty patterns.

"I found these on the beach, I swear," he anticipated her objections, "and I'm taking them home with me."

"But if the customs people find them," Mareike said anxiously, "you'll have to stay here and we'll take off without you."

Despite their squabbling, life without Jochen seemed horrible to her.

"Because of these little things? Never!" Jochen snorted scornfully through his nose. "Besides, I'll hide them carefully."

"Where?" Mareike wanted to know.

"That I won't tell you. Girls can't keep a secret," he said, and Mareike hit him hard in the stomach.

One day, they took a trip to Mombasa. The seaport was about ten kilometers from their hotel, and they took the public bus that stopped nearby.

"I hope we won't catch anything here," Mother whispered softly in the overcrowded bus, where they were pressed together, standing and sitting. She looked at the passengers' tightly curled shiny hair that had strong scents of oils and ointments. Some of the people appeared unclean and shabby and had only torn rags on their bodies, and Mother's concern about vermin did not seem entirely pointless.

"So what," said Jochen drily. "No louse can survive our nightly incense smoke."

He was referring to the fumigating sticks that they had bought on the advice of other hotel guests and which they burned every evening before going to bed. They produced a sweetish smoke which the mosquitoes evidently didn't appreciate. At any rate, it gave them respite for several hours. It's just that they had to endure the smell of the smoldering sticks. But they had to overcome the pests somehow so they wouldn't have to scratch all night. The spinning ventilators in the wall chased away some of the bugs, but the noise they made was worse than the smell of the fumigating sticks.

They could also go on a rampage in the evening and squash all the mosquitoes with a folded newspaper, and Jochen and Father did that a few times, but Mother was such an animal lover that she felt sorry for the dead bugs, and the small blood spots left on the wall were not a pretty sight for anyone.

"These are all mosquito-mothers," she said. "They suck our blood as food for the development of their descendants."

"Now I'm getting emotional," said Father, to whom the mosquito females were most attracted, so that he was always covered with bites. "Must I become baby food for these awful insects?"

And he went on swatting vigorously with the newspaper. Most of the time he didn't hit anything.

So maybe they were also going to bring back lice and fleas from the bus. But they didn't care and had even forgotten all about it by the time they got to Mombasa. The city was throbbing with life and activity. They didn't know where to look and visit first. Above the main street two enormous elephant tusks formed a gate for automobiles and donkey carts.

"Artificial," was Jochen's expert opinion. "There aren't any giant elephant tusks like that."

"But pretty," Mareike said, and Father immediately took a picture of the white arch, the palm trees lining the street, and the big red flowers growing in tubs. The people also were a lively, colorful sight. Most of the native women wrapped Kangas over their hips, which were large skirt-like shawls of multicolored patterns. They wore T-shirts or blouses the same as Europeans, and their hair was covered by colored scarves slung over their heads.

Feet were bare or in simple sandals of only a sole and a leather strap. They had already noticed that on the beach, where the young vendors running around offered again and again to swap one elephant for a pair of plastic sandals. But so far Mother had remained adamant. ·

"You need the shoes because of the heat in the sand and the corals in the water. One the last day, you can give them away if you like."

Here in the streets of Mombasa they were also constantly approached by vendors who had set up their stalls along the sidewalks. Here, too, there were mounds of wood carvings.

"They are really dirt cheap," Jochen observed, "when I think how much they cost at home."

"So you see who pockets the real profit," Father said. "Certainly not the manufacturers of these things here in Africa."

"It's exactly the same with fruits and vegetables," Mother added. "In winter they charge us almost ten marks per pound for Kenyan beans—it's simply crazy to buy them—and the farmers here get barely ten percent of that. They explained that one day on television."

"Look how they make the carvings black," said Jochen, pointing at a man who crouched behind his stall and was daubing a light-colored wooden figure with a little brush. By his side, he had a small jar that looked like a can of shoe polish.

"And then they tell us it is authentic ebony," Mother exclaimed and laughed.

Mareike already knew that ebony is a very

dark wood, shining black, growing wild. After all, trees couldn't be daubed with shoe polish.

Another vendor offered stone figures carved in a white-reddish material. It felt smooth and cool when they took a froglike figure in their hands. The vendor immediately sensed a possible sale.

"English, American, German?" he tried to determine their nationality, and when Mareike said unabashedly, "German," he unleashed a torrent of German gibberish.

"You, you pretty girl. You buy this animal, cheap, cheap, cheap. You me make happy."

They had to laugh, and Mother asked softly, "Do you really want this animal?"

"Oh, yes, please," Mareike pleaded, and Mother whispered, "But then let me haggle, we have to do that here,"

"How much?" she asked, and when the Black man stated the price she turned up her eyes and pretended.

"Much too expensive, me poor woman with many children."

"You beautiful woman, beautiful children," the man replied, and he laughed because he could see through her play-acting.

"After that compliment, you can't really say no," Father grinned.

"You must bide your time," Mother said, "this is much too soon."

"Stop, halt please," Mareike shouted. "Here is something prettier."

She reached for an animal that looked like a crouching cat. The stone was almost white with only light gray stripes.

"This one looks like Lollipop," she begged. "That's the one I want, please."

The humorous haggling started all over again with much rolling of eyes, laughing, and moaning, until they had brought down the price of the little artifact by one third.

"One half would probably still be a fair price," Mother said, "but the young man was so amusing that I am paying for that, too."

They swapped money and stone cat, and continued on their way.

"What nonsense, these fantasy prices and the long haggling for each item," Jochen said, but Mother and Mareike found it very amusing. There were also real stores with display windows.

"I'm sure the prices shown in here are fixed prices," Father assumed. "They certainly don't haggle a long time in the pharmacy here."

"Otherwise the patient might croak in the meantime," Jochen joked.

Then they bought a green-yellow Kanga shawl for Mother.

"I can use that as a tablecloth for the garden table," she said, "and it costs only eight marks."

"And at carnival time you can wear it and go as a Mombasa belle," Father suggested.

"All right, if you will go as Masai warrior, with loincloth and spear," Mother replied.

They finally bought a Masai spear for Jochen. It was made of black wood decorated with silver wire and colored glass beads, and he proudly carried it through the streets.

In their tour, worked out in advance with the help of their travel guide, they now arrived at the harbor. There they wanted to visit "Fort Jesus," a defiant castle with towers and cannons. Mother read from the guide book:

"In 1528 the Portuguese conquered the city of Mombasa. Half a century later, the Turk, Ali Bei, chased them out again, but they returned with an army of hired man-eating Zimbas and recaptured the city."

"Man-eaters?" Mareike asked, horrified. "There were man-eaters here?"

"That's what it says here," Mother replied, "but that was long ago. I am reading on: 'The Portuguese took over the city again. They built the massive fortification "Fort Jesus"—before which we are now standing—and remained for one hundred years. Then they were besieged and starved out by Arabs from Oman'—no, I can't read any more; this is too horrible."

"There must have been quite some action here," Jochen said, looking at the cannons that stood alongside the fort and were pointed at the ocean.

"I'm glad those days are over," Mareike said, and she shuddered despite the heat.

"Here, maybe," Jochen said, "but there are still plenty of countries where there is hunger and war."

"But no man-eating," Mareike insisted.

"Who knows? The Papuans in New Guinea supposedly still practice cannibalism," Jochen said, "That's what I read in a magazine."

"Well, these magazines often write a lot of nonsense." Mother tried to end that discussion. "Let's not spoil our day with such thoughts." But Jochen wasn't finished.

"You're the one who started it. It's always the kids who are criticized because they watch violent

TV programs, and here it is Mother's travel guide that goes on about these things."

"But it only describes historical facts." Mother looked to Father for help. "This is simply factual information, not entertainment."

"And what about the Karl May stories I received from Grandpa?" Jochen wouldn't let go. "You should read how scalping is described in detail in these novels."

"Well, I hope that my big clever son can judge such matters critically," Mother said weakly, and Father whispered, "Subtle, how you do your educating."

Jochen didn't hear that. He had already run ahead to a corner where several men were squatting on the ground.

"Look, they're playing a board game with bottle caps," he called back to them.

"I want to photograph that," Father said.

"But first ask them nicely whether they don't mind." Mother reminded him. "You know that's the custom here. Muslims, particularly, do not like to have their faces photographed."

"OK, OK," Father said, and started a friendly conversation, using English and sign language.

They took a lot of photographs that day—Jochen had also brought his camera—but they always tried not to point their lenses directly at people's faces. Children presented laughing faces when they saw the cameras and held out their hand to get a few shillings.

Finally Mother sighed, "Now I need something to drink. The terrace of the Castle Hotel is supposed to be best." They all agreed because they were thirsty and exhausted, and the sun was straight above them.

"Back to Moi Avenue," Mother said. "There it is."

"You always use so many foreign words," Mareike complained, "and I don't understand them."

"It's simply the name of the main street with the gate of elephant tusks," Mother explained. "Moi is the president of Kenya and the street is named after him. His full name is Daniel Arap Moi, and the Avenue is a word for street in English and French."

"I knew that," Jochen said. In ninth grade he had started taking French in addition to English and Latin."

"Then say so the next time," Mareike snapped, "so I don't have to ask so much."

She was moody, and stayed that way when they sat on the covered terrace. The Coke was lukewarm because her parents did not want her to have ice cubes. "We're expressly warned about that because the water tends to give us Europeans diarrhea."

They had not been allowed to order ice cream for the same reason—only a piece of cake that was much too sweet. Also, Mareike didn't feel comfortable because a lot of wretched figures had gathered around the terrace. Beggars watched in silence as the guests ate; they stretched out their hands imploringly. They were apparently not allowed to enter the terrace because the waiters were constantly shooing them away with hissed instructions, but they couldn't be thrust away entirely.

Near them there stood a white-haired old man whose wrinkled brown face held large dead eyes, like white-blue globes.

"Look, Mommy, this man is blind," Mareike said. "Why doesn't anyone take care of him?"

"I'm sure somebody does," Mother replied. "Here, too, they have hospitals and charitable organizations."

"But I feel so sorry for him," said Mareike, and almost started crying.

Apparently their conversation had been overheard at the next table, because a heavy man wearing a Hawaiian shirt and shorts turned toward them.

"Don't worry, young lady," he said in a deep, friendly bass voice. "The people aren't that bad off here. These beggars are organized bands that always send forward the most miserable-looking one, an old man, a cripple, or a child. At night they get together and share the money."

"But it's very sad if they need that," Mother said, "to have to beg for their daily bread."

"Their daily bread is booze," the stranger said. "don't feel sorry for them. They're all crooks."

"But look at that one over there," Mareike cried, and pointed to a woman lying on the sidewalk. "What's wrong with her?"

They all looked over there—Jochen, the parents, and also the man at the next table.

"Appears to have no legs," he said. "She can only crawl."

"What?" shouted Mareike, who was feeling sick. "A woman without legs has to lie here in the dirt?"

"In our country they have wheelchairs or at least crutches," Jochen said indignantly. "And for the wheelchair users, we have ramps and low-mounted pay phones."

"She had a child on her back," Mother said in consternation. "Look, she has tied it under the shawl."

The child, a baby about six months old, clung to its mother's back as she propelled herself slowly forward on her belly. She pulled forward with her

Mombasa residence

Marketplace

A Masai

Basket maker

Migwani woman

A donkey is used to carry water.

Left: The new house
Right: The old house

Migwani schoolroom

Children

Migwani women

School children of Migwani

Dear mrs Gantenbein　　　　　　　　6302301/00128

　　Greetings and best wishes to you I
Phope you are fine. I too am doing well although
missed school for one week after we reopened I was hit
ou the Leg by a tree branch and I couldut walk to school
I have now recovered and I have started school again I
did ne miss alot because the holidas had Just ended and
the children were settling in their new class rooms. I
am now in grade 5 and I am happy to be going higher
every year. I will have to work hard How are the rest. Kiss
the children happy new year for me. I have at last

recievd the birth day gift you had talked of in your last Letter
I was very happy and grateful about it I bought clothing
for myself and my mother too. we both were very grateful
to you my God bless you and increase your generosity.
you always make me feel happy and I love you my sister and
brother who are older than me are going to training.

my sister wants to do dress making and my brother capentry.

Pray for them to work hard. Last week we ate fresh beans
from our garden we enjoyed them unfortunately they
wont last till harvest time because they are very few and
weu finish them when they are still in the gaden. All the
the best for a happy 1984!

　　Yours Alice　Ilai

A letter from Alice

Alice

powerful arms. Her legs did appear to be stumps without feet.

"This is ghastly," Mother said. "How can we help?"

"Give me money, please," Mareike said. "I'll give it to her."

"The beggars will descend on you like vultures," Father warned.

"I don't care," Mareike said, and Mother had already grabbed her purse.

"Here, take a handful," she said, and pressed the coins into Mareike's hand. "Maybe that will bring her a little joy."

Mareike clutched the coins and without looking around she quickly walked to the opposite sidewalk.

"Jambo," she said to the woman on the ground. The woman interrupted her slow crawl and looked with astonishment at the little foreign girl. She still had a young face, but large sad eyes. The baby on her back looked like her. Flies were crawling through its curly hair.

"Jambo," Mareike said again, and held out the coins. The woman propped herself up with her left hand, extended the right one and took the money. "Assante," she said softly, and stuck it somewhere in her Kanga. Then she braced herself again on both arms and continued to crawl.

Mareike turned around fast so she wouldn't have to bawl, and she returned with bowed head to the table.

"I understand you, dear," Mother said, and stroked Mareike arm. "It's hardly bearable."

They sat in silence for a while and drank their lukewarm Coke.

"Well, we knew that there is much poverty and

misery in Africa," Father said finally. "That's, after all, why we sponsored a child."

"Thank you for reminding us," Mother said forcefully. "Now I'm going to take action to get to Alice."

"What in the world will you do?" her husband asked. "We have to wait for information from the Organization in Nairobi."

"We could ask in the offices of our travel agency what can be done," Mother pleaded. "It's not far from here."

"Yes, let's go," Mareike agreed. She was not happy on the terrace of the elegant hotel, surrounded by lurking beggars. She needed to move about.

"All right, if that's what you want to do, but without detailed travel instructions we will never find Migwani."

"But that's what these people are here for, to help us tourists," Mother said. "They must surely have accurate maps."

They paid the waiter and wound their way through the city with their map. The travel agency's office was easy to find; the store window displayed the same logo that appeared on their travel documents and luggage tags.

The office was pleasantly dark and cool, and a polite young man offered to assist them. But it was not Johnny, who had met them at the airport. Brinkmeyer, he introduced himself. The opposite of Meierbrink, thought Mareike—let's hope that isn't a bad omen.

"We want to get to Migwani," Mother said simply, "to visit our godchild."

"Migwani?" the young man repeated. "Never heard of it."

"It's a village in Kitui province which you must certainly be familiar with."

"At any rate it's not an area visited by tourists," the young man said, and pulled out a map.

"You will find it difficult to get there. You see, there is no train line. There's a road that leads to Kitui, but that's the end."

"How about using a car?" Father suggested.

"If you think you can do it," Mr. Brinkmeyer said. Another agent joined them and shook his head skeptically.

"It would be better to use a native driver who can ask directions."

The daily rate he cited for a rental car with driver was so high that the parents exchanged a startled look.

"Or a small charter plane ..."

"You don't even have to tell us the price of that," Father interrupted him. "It's out of the question."

"Well, you can get as far as Nairobi by train. The question is how to proceed from there."

"But I have no precise information," Mother said dejectedly. "The Organization is simply not responding."

"That's the African view of life," Mr. Brinkmeyer's colleague said. "They take their time here. Why don't you call them?"

"Could I do this from here with your help?" Mother asked, and looked at him pleadingly. "I will pay for the call, of course."

"OK, let's try. We do want to help our customers when we can. Do you have the telephone number?"

Naturally, Mother had not brought it along. But there was an information service in Mombasa, and they found the number of the Organization. Mr Brinkmeyer dialed, and Mareike crossed her fingers hard: Please, let us succeed, she begged some helpful spirit in Africa or elsewhere. We must get to Alice.

And her plea was heard. Mr. Brinkmeyer spoke rapid English with someone at the other end and then handed the receiver to Mother with a smile.

"They are connecting you to the director of the Organization. You can tell her your problem."

Mother wiped beads of sweat from her forehead, although the office was quite cool, and seized the receiver with a slightly trembling hand.

"Hello," she said again and again, "hello, hello," Of the conversation that followed, Mareike understood only her own family name, the word Germany, and the word Alice.

Mother stuttered a little and her voice grew louder a few times, but finally she said "thank you" in English and hung up.

"She says they will have a car available on Monday and can get us to Migwani," she said in an uncertain voice. "We are to report to the Organization office. I have the address."

"This was so simple, all of a sudden," Father said with surprise.

"Yes, there didn't seem to be any problem. This week godparents from England were visiting, and that's why they had no time for us."

"Is Alice all right?" Mareike wanted to know.

"She said nothing about that; she must have hundreds of children in her card file and cannot possibly know them all." Mother still looked somewhat disconcerted.

"How is this going to work? And how are we going to get to Nairobi in the morning?"

"That's no problem," said Mr. Brinkmeyer, who looked more and more like a guardian angel to them. "You will take the night train from Mombasa, which gets to Nairobi at seven a.m."

"Well, then we have to wait till Sunday and leave in the evening," Mother said, half-affirmatively, half-questioningly. "This waiting is terrible."

"Meanwhile, how would you like to join one of our short safaris?" Mr. Brinkmeyer asked cordially. "Right now we can offer you a reasonably priced three-day safari to the Tsavo National Park, and you could be back by Saturday."

"Isn't that very expensive?" asked Mother, who was not shy about discussing money and who wanted to have enough left over for the trip to Kitui.

But the price quoted to them was not high, and Father said, "We should do that. We'll see something of the country and won't wear out our nerves waiting."

"Will we see wild animals, then?" Jochen wanted to know.

"But of course," Mr. Brinkmeyer beamed, "giraffes, elephants, buffaloes, lions—our drivers are very familiar with the territory and drive their jeeps right among them."

"And where do we spend the night? In tents?" Mother asked with apprehension.

"No, in lodges. They are comfortable little hotels right on the steppe."

"Right in the midst of all the animals?" Jochen looked excited.

"Yes, of course, they're so close you can almost touch them."

Mr. Brinkmeyer's colleague looked at Mareike.

"Are three days in a jeep going to be too tiring for the young lady?"

"I can handle that," Mareike said with indignation. "I can stand heat and thirst better than anyone."

She thought of some hotel guests who spent their days lying in the shadow of the palm trees and were always asking for the next cold drink.

"She's right," Father, Mother, and Jochen said at the same time, and Mareike looked proudly at the two young men in their air-conditioned office.

"Well, here is a brochure that describes the safari in detail," Mr Brinkmeyer said with a smile. "Please make your reservations as early as possible."

They shook hands and went out again into the hot African sun, full of this new idea and ready for action.

They wanted to take a taxi back to the hotel. This had been a long and exhausting day. Many colorful cars with varying numbers of dents and broken windows were stopped by the sidewalk. They didn't look at all like the taxis at home. As the family walked along, hesitating and searching, the drivers immediately sniffed possible customers and turned to Mother with an expectant grin, "Taxi, madame? Fine Mercedes?"

"If that's a Mercedes I don't know anything about cars," Jochen mumbled, checking out a boldly patched crate with different colored fenders. "Why do they always address their offers to Mother?"

"With the instinct of the primitive man, they sense who is the head of our family," Father laughed, and Mother poked him in the ribs.

"They are courteous and want to put the woman at ease," she snapped. "And anyway: in Africa women are highly respected and are very important."

"Yes, I read that too in the travel guide," said Father, still laughing, "but only because they do all the work in the fields and in the home. All right, deluxe woman, which car do you want to take?"

Mother opted for a bright red one that also looked fairly clean. After they got in, they noticed that that was not so, and that the cushions with their ancient springs were hard on their fannies. Also, the windshield wiper started all of a sudden during the ride and wouldn't stop despite the radiant sunshine. But they were grateful for the fast ride back to their hotel.

They spent the evening poring over the travel agency brochure. Jochen preferred a one-week safari deep into West Kenya, all the way to the Serengeti with its famous large animal reserves. But that safari took too much time and cost too much.

"We have to take the train to Nairobi on Sunday," Mother reminded them. "I vote for the three-day trip by jeep. That will take us through the Tsavo National Park and the Amboseli Park, where there are also all kinds of animals."

"Are those really parks?" Mareike asked. "With benches and kiosks?"

"Certainly not," Father explained. "They are nature preservation areas, where gamekeepers stand guard to protect the wild animals from being shot. In past decades and centuries, many animals have been exterminated, and now they are doing quite a bit in Kenya to protect nature. Remember the shells we're not allowed to take out of the country?"

"But can we run around there?"

Father shook his head, thinking. "I don't know. Among lions and elephants? We'll see. I think Mother's right. We should call the travel agency early tomorrow morning to make our reservations."

"And then we get going day after tomorrow between five and six o'clock," Jochen read aloud out of the brochure.

"Good lord, let's stock up on sleep then," Mother ordered. "Off to bed with you. And don't forget to light the fumigating sticks."

Mareike dreamed a lot about wild animals that night, but her dreams weren't scary—they were amusing. The elephants and rhinoceroses allowed themselves to be petted, and when a giraffe approached, a furry animal was clinging to its neck; it looked an awful lot like Lollipop, the tomcat. Lolli, come down, Mareike cried in her dream, but that's when she woke and heard Mother calling, "Breakfast, children, come and get it."

Father settled everything about the excursion by telephone, and they started right away to pack two travel bags with the necessities: pajamas, cameras, T-shirts and changes of underwear, ointments for bugs and sunburn.

"I can't possibly get sunburned," Jochen assured them. "I've been running around in the sun all day."

The jeep and driver arrived the next morning when it was still pitch-dark. Mother really had to wake the children. They had talked in bed for a long while the night before because they were too excited to sleep, so they had had only four hours of sleep. They did a minimum of washing with a lot of growling and grumbling, and then gulped the tea that Mother prepared in the kitchen nook, which was now practically free of ants. They swallowed two or three bananas, and they were ready for action.

The jeep had seats for eight, but since they were first, they could choose the ones they wanted. They took the seats right behind the driver.

"Achmed," he introduced himself, and they could see despite the very dim light from the front door that he was grinning.

The night was still coal-black, and Mareike was startled again when tall, dark hotel guards stepped out of the bushes with their nightsticks. But they only wanted to help them into the car and make sure that the little cottage was safely locked. Their parents informed the hotel management that they would be away for three days.

Achmed drove like a racing driver, and by the time they reached the very first stop sign near the hotel, they had already been shaken as though on a roller coaster, But at least it woke them up. Only Mother looked a little nauseated and nervous.

"Is this the way it's going to be?" she asked Father. "I can't take it for three days."

"Later on we'll be driving on a lovely, straight and smooth road," said one of the two new passengers who had taken the seats behind them. "We have taken this trip before and are somewhat familiar with it. Müller," they introduced themselves, "from Berlin."

They were a nice older couple, and the children immediately plied them with questions about everything they were about to see.

They didn't divulge much. "Wait and see," they smiled. "It is different every time. Sometimes you're lucky and can observe an entire lion family, sometimes only zebras."

"Oh, that would be enough for me," Mareike said, "an entire herd of zebras, that must be awesome!"

"Right you are," said old Mr. Müller, and looked at her with pleasure, "but there are some tourists who collect excitement and shoot pictures like big game hunters used to do with their guns. They are not satisfied if they haven't seen all the animals that are listed in the travel guide, and they check them off as they see them."

"That's dumb," Jochen said, "just like those Americans who race through Europe and do it all in eight days."

The last two passengers appeared to be of that sort. They were a young couple in overly elegant getups. The young man carried a camcorder on his shoulder, and the young woman wore Western boots with rivets and spurs and an imitation leopard suit.

Brother and sister had to giggle, but Mother gave them a warning look and they didn't say anything.

It was still dark outside when they drove through Mombasa. Only a few street lamps were dimly lit. But a few people were already hurrying through the streets, carrying bundles on their heads and in their arms. Mareike admired again how the women were able to balance heavy loads—baskets and even jugs—on their heads and how erect and gracefully they walked. She had once tried that with a large book, and had dropped it after only a few steps. She found that the women in this country were exceptionally pretty. Coffee-colored skin, short black curls—which, in the case of little girls, were decorated with gay, colorful ribbons—and these beautifully controlled body movements. As they sashayed in their colorful shawls reaching down to the ankles, some of them looked simply regal.

After Mombasa, they got onto a smooth paved road, and Mother managed to relax again. And then the sun rose, fast and abruptly, like every morning at six o'clock, and they had a wide, wide view of the country.

Right and left of the road, the ground was red earth in which agave leaves grew straight up like so many spears. From time to time, there appeared trees with umbrella-like tops and, like everywhere, dry bushes with many thorns. In the background, on could see softly rolling mountain chains with the road leading toward them like a bright ribbon.

Achmed was singing a mysterious-sounding song from back of his throat. From time to time he turned toward his passengers and asked, "Fine?" and they all nodded.

It was not just "fine," it was awe-inspiring. Up to now, they had only seen the dense green coastline around Mombasa, where the vegetation was green and lush owing to the constant moisture from the ocean. Now they were entering the steppe, and the could now picture what was meant by dryness and parched fields in the reports about Alice and her homeland. There were not even any fields here, and no human habitation as far as the eye could see.

"What are these?" cried Jochen suddenly, pointing at red, meter-high heaps at the road's edge that looked like the sand castles children build on ocean beaches. But these were two or three meters high, with many towers and battlements. He asked the same question in English, and Achmed responded with a torrent of words. Jochen glanced helplessly at his mother, who tried to interpret.

"These are termite hills," she said. "You know, like the giant ant hills in our forests."

"And they build that all by themselves?" Mareike asked in amazement.

"Who is going to help them? Some earth spirit, no doubt?" Jochen was joshing his younger sister once again, and she responded by calling him "bonehead" and kicking his shins.

The young man on the rear bench was already pointing his camcorder and yelling, "Stop!" but Achmed did not stop and assured them laughingly that there would be many more and that he would stop later in Tsavo Park.

Mother, still feeling a little dizzy, was pleased when he did stop at a gas station that suddenly materialized along the road. While he filled up, they were able to go to the toilet and pick up something to eat at the snack bar. There were already jeeps there, and they were besieged by vendors offering animal wood carvings.

"Much cheaper than in Mombasa," Jochen soon discovered, and he pestered until Father bought him an elephant, black with white tusks.

"I hope it isn't real ivory," he said, and Mareike learned that ivory was actually elephant tusks. These had always been in great demand and they used to carve jewelry out of them that acquired a lovely golden hue with age. Mr Müller told them that many elephants had been killed just for their tusks and that they had often lost their lives in a most cruel manner. But now this was forbidden, at least in Kenya, at least officially. But there were still poachers around. On TV you could sometimes see horrible pictures of killed elephants with gaping wounds where the tusks had been.

"But this looks like plastic," Mother said.

Mr. Müller had the facts. "The body is made of stained wood, the tusks of bone. You can safely take this with you, it's a good piece of work."

"I'll give this to Grandpa," Jochen said. "He'll certainly like it, with his love of adventure stories."

They soon reached the nature conservation area proper. It was indeed not a park with a fence, but a large gate with a guard did indicate where it started.

There were more trees and bushes here, but the ground still appeared dry and dusty, and the tufts of grass were parched yellow. No sooner had they driven through the gate than they saw their first elephant.

"That one isn't real," Father said. "They mounted him there to greet the tourists."

"You mean like in the recreation park near Cologne?" Mareike asked.

"He's moving, he is real!" Jochen roared, and the young man aimed his camcorder.

Achmed had stopped willingly and was grinning to himself.

"There will be many, many more," he kept saying, but to his passengers this first elephant in liberty naturally caused great excitement.

"Couldn't he trample us?" Mother asked.

"Maybe," Father said, "but why should he? Animals attack only if provoked. That differentiates them from human beings."

Mr. Müller joined in the discussion in his friendly and calm manner. "They won't do anything," he declared. "They know the jeeps. Besides, these are painted black and white and look like big zebras to them."

"Oh, that's why," Mareike said. "I've been wondering why the car is painted that way."

"The one thing we must not do is leave the vehicle," warned Mrs. Müller. "After all, they are not domestic animals, and lions may be lurking behind many bushes."

Achmed drove on slowly, and they stretched their necks in all directions not to miss anything. It was getting hot in the jeep.

Achmed raised the roof so they could stand up, get a better view and snap pictures. Father and Jochen had long since prepared their cameras, and both had photographed the first large elephant.

"Giraffes," Mother shouted. "There to our right!" and they all spun around. Three, four, five giraffes were running slow and tall over the steppe, their legs moving smoothly as if in slow motion.

"Stop, stop, stop!" shouted Jochen, Father and the camcorder man.

Achmed said again, "Come many, many more," but he did slow down.

"If he stops for every animal we'll never reach the lodge today," Mr. Müller said with a smile, "but in one or two hours the excitement will have cooled, and we will all become used to the spectacle."

"Well, I find it exciting and wonderful," Mareike said, and discovered a group of strange tall birds standing around in a group.

"Those are secretaries," Mr. Müller said.

"I always though that referred to office employees or writing desks," Father laughed.

"Well, look at them, don't they just stand there, drab and dignified, like some old office managers?"

He was right, the secretary birds did look like distinguished old gentlemen. By contrast, the zebras, which they observed a little later, looked like children playing in their pajamas. They soon did not know where to look first, there was so much to see.

Achmed drove them slowly over narrow sandy paths, and he did stop from time to time, but not as often by far as the eager photographers would have liked. "Come many, many more," he would say every time Jochen or the camcorder man protested. Meanwhile there were many jeeps around, and whenever several of them stopped in a circle, one knew there was something particularly interesting to see.

Mother was sitting there with shining eyes. One could actually sense how she was storing the images in memory even without a camera. In winter she would give another slide lecture before her women's club and describe things that the others had long since forgotten. Mareike tried to follow her example and simply observe and remember. But, still, she regretted a little not having her own camera. That's what she should have wished for for Christmas instead of books, which were only paper, after all, and not real life.

Around noon, when the heat became unbearable, Achmed drove toward a group of trees behind which there soon appeared a couple of low wooden buildings.

"Kilaguni Lodge," he said. "Fine lunch."

He mixed English and German words, but they all understood him.

"Great," they all exclaimed, since they had not been allowed to leave the car all morning. The cans of soda and rolls of fruit drops were all gone, and they looked forward to some refreshments.

But what they found in the lodge surpassed their expectations. The small hotel's dining room was air-conditioned, and the most delicious food one could imagine was laid out on several self-service counters. They could take all the salad, fruit, grilled sausage, and cake they wanted, and waiters in white coats served any drink they desired.

"How do they get this over here?" Mother wondered, and Mr. Müller told them about the enormous effort the country was exerting to attract tourists and earn hard currency.

"And yet everything is inexpensive," said Father. He had paid a lump-sum check at the door for the whole family, and they were now reveling in all the delicacies.

Jochen naturally finished first because he wanted to explore the hotel. He quickly came back.

"Would you believe?" he crowed. "They have a swimming pool here."

"Yes, they always build the lodges where there are springs and a well can be dug," explained Mr. Müller. "Tonight we will stop and spend the night at another one where there is a big animal watering hole. We will be able to observe how they come there to drink."

"But isn't all this luxury and wastefulness," Mother said pensively, "when people are hungry and thirsty in other parts of Kenya."

"Sure," said Mr. Müller, shrugging his shoulders. "But what good is this over there? The water cannot be carried there. And our money is valuable hard currency for the country. As far as I know, the government is trying hard and, for example, is building roads in remote areas."

"Well, that's something we will be able to judge," Mother said, and she told the Müllers about Alice. They, too, were skeptical and did not think the visit would really work out.

"Things are well organized here because many tourists come here. But farther north ..."

Jochen kept running from the swimming pool to the cool dining room and back. Mareike rested and listened to the adults. They were to continue very soon. Until dark they would drive through the steppe and would certainly still see a lot. She already felt full of images and would actually have preferred staying there.

When they all got into the jeep again they were overcome by the brutal heat and there was general moaning among the passengers.

Achmed continued to sing unperturbed and to steer the car on paths that only he could see. Suddenly he sat up and said mysteriously, "Simba, simba."

"Lion in sight," Mr. Müller interpreted, and the camcorder man became agitated again. Achmed slowed the jeep down and steered it carefully toward a clump of trees.

For a long time there was nothing to see, but then, "There he lies," Mrs. Müller whispered excitedly, "and there is the lioness, and one or two young ones."

Now the children were able to see them too. A lion family lay drowsily in the shadow of an umbrella acacia. Only the cub was playing with its mother's tail which twitched back and forth. "the king of animals, the lord of the wilderness," Mother whispered.

When they encountered a buffalo herd a little later, Mareike asked for photographs. She liked the buffalo because of their large friendly faces below the hair neatly parted in the middle and the horns diverging like tight braids.

"They aren't as harmless as they look, though,"

the Müllers told them. "When a buffalo herd comes thundering toward a car, it's a very scary thing."

But these buffalo weren't thinking of any thundering attack. They were peacefully grazing.

Achmed was now driving a little faster because they still had to reach their night accommodations. Also, the "stop" calls by the passengers became less frequent. They had shot several rolls and were getting tired.

"Look, the birds are tired, too, and are allowing the buffalo to carry them," Mareike remarked when another large peaceful herd of these animals appeared.

"Those are oxpeckers," she was informed. "They feed on the buffaloes' vermin."

"How convenient," she said. "If our Lolli had such a bird servant, we wouldn't always have to pull those disgusting ticks out his hair."

That was always a tiresome procedure in summer. The bloodsuckers got a firm hold on the hair and filled up on the cat's blood, but when they held firmly to remove the insects, he didn't appreciate it and would scratch and bite.

These insects were also called wood ticks because they live in woods and bushes, and Jochen punned feebly, "Lolli needs a wood tick chopper, —woodchopper for short."

He and Mareike were giggling and talking nonsense. Mother recognized the signs, "You two are exhausted and you belong in bed."

The beds in their overnight quarters were surrounded by white netting. A large curtain of fine white tulle was attached to the ceiling and opened downward like an umbrella or tent, shrouding the entire bed.

"That's a mosquito net," the parents explained. "You can sleep soundly under that, and the insects won't get you."

"Unless one of them should crawl under the net," Jochen said skeptically, "and get tangled up in it."

During the "trial lying in" that the brother and sister immediately organized they both got tangled up in it and Jochen almost tore the mosquito net from the ceiling.

"Good grief," he said. "I'll have to lie stiff and stock-still all night."

"Well, it's better than being devoured by mosquitoes," his sister said sensibly.

"Yes, and there are no air conditioners to chase them away with noise and airflow," Mother remarked.

They also discovered very soon why these mosquito nets were superfluous. It got pretty cold out here in the steppe when night came. Climate and landscape were simply very different here than in the coastline belt around Mombasa. The lodge's small brown wooden cottages were like a homey island in an infinite expanse under a dark blue sky. When the four of them walked back to the main building—Mother and Father were then going to stay in the bar for a while—they looked up breathlessly at that immense celestial dome. The constellations appeared completely different from those at home in Germany, and the color of the night sky was different, too.

"Like velvet," Mother said, and this corny description was exactly right. They stayed still for a moment and let the quiet and the vastness penetrate them. Only from very far could they hear mysterious cries of invisible animals that did not rest even at night. Or maybe it was the last cry of prey pounced upon by a hyena.

Mareike felt a cold shudder down her spine. When the door of the main building opened up and a torrent of sound and stream of light escaped, she was almost relieved.

Dinner was very much like midday lunch at the Kilaguni Lodge, but the children were exhausted and didn't eat much, and they did not protest when Father ordered, "Under the nets, everyone!"

The next morning was bright and radiant like every morning here in Africa. How often they would wake up in the morning in Germany and see a gray-hung rainy sky, even in July. Here they experienced a few short showers in the course of the day, but these were warm, fierce, and lasted only a few minutes. But here in the steppe even these showers didn't seem to exist. Here there was no green except around a few springs and rivers.

They departed quickly, stowing their few things in the travel bags. Achmed awaited them with a beaming smile and the habitual "Jambo." He spoke Kisuaheli, the Black's common language. He himself was an Arab from somewhere in Northern Africa as he vaguely explained. "Kenya big, Kenya beautiful, much work and money," he also said, and he had naturally adapted to the language of the country. German and English he mixed quite freely, owing to the many tourists he drove every day.

The old Müllers were pleasant and friendly like the day before. The young couple had completely changed clothes. Instead of slacks and Western boots they now wore shorts, the young man with a bright multicolored Hawaiian shirt and the young woman a T-shirt with leopard pattern.

"I hope the wild animals won't be jealous and attack our jeep," Father whispered, grinning, and Mother hissed, "Don't look so close."

She was a little pale and tired, but when they stopped for the first group of elephants sauntering across their path she sparkled again.

The landscape changed notably during today's drive. The ground was no longer red dust and dry grassland but black fissured rock.

"This is lava stone," Mr. Müller explained, "residue from the eruption of the Shetani volcano."

"Incidentally, Shetani means Satan," explained his wife.

"Children, you can use your imagination to picture Satan spitting brimstone and fire."

They didn't find the somber landscape surrounding them restful. And when tall slender figures holding long spears in their hands appeared, everything took on an even more foreign and menacing look. The young man started to point his camcorder.

"Psst, no, this be Masai land," hissed Achmed. "Nix photo, make them very angry."

"Why can't we photograph them?" Father asked in English. The picturesque young warriors were tempting snapshot models.

Achmed then explained carefully, as interpreted by Mother, that they would be driving for quite a while through territory that the Masai regarded as their property. While they tolerated the passage of the safari vehicles, they could become very unpleasant if anyone stared at them or photographed them like animals in a zoo.

"They are proud nomads," he concluded, and Mareike recalled the film that Flocke had shown them. If only Flocke were here to see this now.

Achmed explained that they would stop at a Masai village later on. If they gave the village chief a few dollars, they would be allowed to snap pictures, but only there in the village. "They call that a kraal," Mareike commented. She had understood what he was talking about.

"In other words, there's the Wild West and greed here, too," said the young man, who had not talked much up to then because he was too absorbed by his camcorder and his girlfriend.

"The Masai are actually very poor," Mrs. Müller commented, and Mareike nodded her head in agreement. "They have only their cattle herds, and the grazing grounds are shrinking all the time."

"But why don't they move to the cities, to Mombasa, for example?" asked the camcorder man's woman friend.

Mareike was proud that she could give information to the woman who was so much older than she. "They're nomads," she said. "They would be very unhappy if they couldn't wander."

"But don't they go to school at all?" the young woman wanted to know. Mareike didn't know, but when Mother relayed the question to Achmed he told them that the government sent them teachers if they provided a school building. For that and for other things they need money ... "and milk the tourists," Jochen added drily.

Yet, when they finally stopped at a kraal, he was the most insistent to ask Father to pay the "Entrance Fee." It was somewhat expensive but Mother agreed, "We won't have another such opportunity any time soon." And Father gave the bills to an old man who accepted them with a haughty look.

The Müllers stayed with Achmed in the bus since they had already seen and photographed all this on their previous trip, but the young couple came along and the price didn't make them hesitate. How did they manage to have enough money for such a trip at their young age, Mareike wondered, and for a camcorder?

She would have liked to ask how they earned their money, but she didn't dare. Her parents weren't poor either. They had a house and a car and so on, but without Aunt Hedwig's unexpected present they couldn't have afforded this African expedition.

She stormed out behind the others who had already entered the kraal. Through a sort of hedge made of cut-down thorny branches they entered the circle in which the huts stood. They looked like upside-down bowls and surrounded a second circle of thorny branches in which little goats and calves were bleating and lowing.

"Must be the kindergarten," Mother assumed. "The grown animals are over there, outside."

She pointed to a herd of thin brown cattle that were grazing not far from the kraal. A slender young man in a red cape kept watch over them.

Red and red-brown were the dominant colors in the kraal as well. The huts looked like that because the dried cow dung used to build them had been covered with red clay. The hair of most Masai was dyed red, and their capes were the same color. They were standing or sitting in front of their huts and looked blankly, almost condescendingly, at the strangers. The small children were squatting next to their mothers.

An old man leading the six tourists around and finally stopped before a woman holding up an armful of bead jewelry.

"We should buy these," Mother said. "I'd like such a necklace."

"But they look like plastic pearls," Father said warily.

"So what. They were made by hand and created in an authentic Masai kraal," Mother insisted.

Some of the young men were standing there with their spears, looking somber and menacing. They looked as though they wished the tourists would go to the devil.

The woman with the jewelry accepted the money with just a suggestion of a smile. The young couple bought so much junk they could hardly carry it, and Mareike wondered again about the distribution of wealth and poverty in the world. Did these two also have a godchild or would they contribute something if she told them about that? She decided to bring up the subject some time during the safari.

Achmed blew his horn three times and they knew it was time to leave. Conversation with these curious people was impossible anyway, and they couldn't see into their huts because of the low doors. The old man escorted them back to the jeep and lifted his hand briefly in parting. He carried only a stick in his hand, not a spear like the young men, who looked like warriors.

Achmed could not tell them much either about these mysterious people. He now drove very fast so they could have their lunch before the midday heat. They reached a lodge again, comprising several cottages, and the children were enchanted by small monkeys scurrying around in front of the dining hall that trustingly let themselves be fed.

"Be careful, they sometimes bite," said Mrs. Müller, and a loud scream from another child confirmed her warning.

"Save some fruit from your lunch, and throw it to them," Mother said. And that's what they did.

As they were squatting and distributing bananas and orange slices, a big elephant suddenly came stomping toward the lodge, ears flapping.

"I bet he's the guard here," Jochen shouted, and ran to meet him. Everybody started yelling, "Stop, don't, come back" and other words that Jochen did not understand, but he did stop in his tracks. The elephant kept trotting toward him and raised his trunk. Father ran up to Jochen and pulled him back by the arm.

"For God's sake, Jochen, come to the house. The waiters say he's a vicious rogue. He would kill you."

He said this hurriedly in a low voice as they walked back to the house, looking behind them all the while.

"Don't run, don't make a noise, don't provoke him," Father murmured. "Just move slowly, we'll be there right away."

The waiters had already opened the door, and they closed it fast as soon as Father and Jochen were inside. Outside, everyone had disappeared, even the monkeys.

The elephant stopped, looked with his cunning eyes at the humans behind the glass pane, and swung his trunk around.

"He isn't going to break in here, is he?" Mother asked fearfully.

"That's unlikely," said Mr. Müller standing next to her. "He's not going to want to crash through the glass pane."

The giant animal didn't seem tempted to do that. He turned around, dropped two big elephant pats, as if to show his contempt, and ambled away, ears waving.

"My heavens," Mother was very pale. "Jochen, we were lucky this time."

"But I could have run away from him," he replied without much assurance.

"Do you have any idea how fast elephants can run?" said Mr Müller. "And don't forget his trunk. It has a long reach and can toss a young boy like you into the air."

"I once saw that at the circus," Mareike said. "Oh boy, Jochen, that would have been awesome."

"You heartless little worm," he replied, and the squabble that followed made them forget all the excitement.

Because of the scare, they lingered a bit during lunch until Achmed appeared to remind them. "Must get to Amboseli today," he said. "Fine lodge, fine dinner, many, many animals."

In fact, they did see many, many animals that afternoon, but after a while they all put down their cameras, became very quiet, and merely looked out the window.

The Amboseli Lodge was as attractive and comfortable as the ones they had already visited. Its particular feature was a broad terrace with a good view of the watering place. After nightfall they were able to observe from the terrace how the animals came to the water's edge, and they all forgot their fatigue, even the children.

The water hole was faintly lit by cleverly hidden projectors, and they could clearly see the hyenas and jackals sneaking cautiously like large dogs or foxes, quickly jumping back into the darkness at every sound.

"Hush," everybody on the terrace was reminded when glasses clinked.

Then the animals drank in long, thirsty gulps, and disappeared as suddenly as they had appeared.

Suddenly everyone on the terrace became even more quiet when someone whispered, "Simba, a lion." Mareike watched with bated breath as the animal advanced stealthily. The slow, lithe movements of a feline. Just like Lolli when he tries to catch a fly, she thought, and barely suppressed a giggle.

The lion had now reached its goal and was drinking calmly. Just like Lolli when he laps his warm evening milk, she again thought, and all of a sudden she felt great nostalgia for her home and its familiar surroundings.

The next morning they were off again, right after breakfast. They drove through the nature conservation area for a while, but then Achmed turned onto the big, wide road that led directly back to Mombasa. The road came from Nairobi, and when Mareike heard that, she thought with a throbbing heart, Nairobi, we must already have been near Alice...

Mother must have had a similar thought, because she was looking down at her lap instead of watching the landscape.

"Tomorrow we'll be on our way, right?" she asked, and Mother knew right away what she meant and nodded to her with a smile. The return trip was long and somewhat monotonous. The road stretched like an endless gray ribbon over the landscape they were already familiar with, and there were hardly any animals to be seen. During this ride Mareike got to find out a little more about the young couple with the camcorder. The conversation had turned to the lodges where they had had their meals and spent their nights, and how surprising it was to find such comfort out here in the steppe. The "camcorder man" then told them that his parents also ran a large restaurant.

"And a disco that is visited by teenagers like you," he added, looking at Jochen.

"I don't go to discos." Jochen was almost offended. "I've just completed a dancing school and I can really dance. In the discos they just jump around."

"OK," the young man said with a grin. "But for most youngsters the important thing is they can meet girls there."

Jochen, who had written almost every evening to his dance class friend—this had to be something like love—did not reply.

Father inquired courteously about how such a restaurant is run, but Mareike noticed that he wasn't really interested. He just wanted to be sociable. Then she burst out, "Tomorrow we're going to visit my Black sister." And since the old Müllers and the young couple looked at her in amazement, she added, "Yes, our godchild in Kitui."

That gave them a topic of conversation until they reached Mombasa. The young people reacted with the same rubbish the Meierbrinks had expressed when they visited that evening: it's all a sham, who knows where the godparents' money goes, etc.

Mareike gave up all hope of extracting a charitable contribution from them for the Organization despite all the money they had for travel and the camcorder. But the old Müllers were genuinely interested and wrote down the addresses Mother gave them.

"If you return from your expedition to Kitui and confirm that everything is on the up and up, I'll send a contribution to the Organization," Mr. Müller promised, and Mareike found him even more likable than before.

"We're a little too old to assume a sponsorship. We don't know how much longer we are still going to live, and such a child requires care for many years."

Mother assured them that any contribution was welcome, since it was all placed in one pool and entire families were being helped, not just individual children.

"There are other organizations that will select a gifted child, send it to school in the nearest city in the hope that after it had been educated, it will return to help its people," she said. "But meanwhile things might be very hard for the rest of the family, and the child may lose contact with its parents. I don't think that is as good a solution as the approach used by our Organization."

The Müllers knew about an SOS children's village near Mombasa, where they took care of destitute children without parents or family.

Somehow the lovely mood of the safari had dissipated. In the last few days they had been concerned with interesting animals and beautiful landscapes. They had almost forgotten the human beings. But when Achmed stopped at a gas station where cute little monkeys tumbled on the car roofs— including their jeep's roof—the children laughed again. They still had some fruit from breakfast and tried to distribute it fairly. But a particularly fresh young female monkey managed to grab a whole banana that Mareike was about to peel and break up. And as gratitude she also scratched Mareike's hand. Mareike stuck the sore thumb in her mouth and sucked it like a lollipop.

When Achmed had finished filling up and saw the little wound, he smiled and took out his first-aid kit.

"Nix bad, monkey clean," he said, and put a few drops of a burning liquid on the cut. Then he wound a long white bandage around her thumb, which was now three times its normal size. Mareike proudly held her hand high and felt like a wounded adventurer after a real safari.

When they reached Mombasa, Father gave Achmed a big tip, and they all thanked him with a handshake for his friendliness and safe driving. Jochen quickly took a picture of Achmed and the Müllers and the young couple, who all posed in front of the jeep.

Meanwhile, the ants had reestablished their presence in their little cottage at the Giriama Apartments.

After lavish showers, they all collapsed into their beds and forgot all about ants, mosquitoes, lions, or monkeys. Mareike's thumb didn't even hurt anymore, but she intended to parade the bandage next morning in the dining room, and kept it on.

In fact, the next morning every other person did ask the nice little girl what had happened to her on the safari. At first Mareike enjoyed it when Jochen invented crazy stories about wild monkeys who had shaken hands with her, or a hyena whose prey his sister had tried to grab.

"You should have seen how both of them were pulling at the bird, the hyena on one side, my sister on the other. Fortunately it didn't feel anything because it was already dead. But Mareike wanted to teach the wild animals some manners."

But when the hyena became a lion in Jochen's next version of the story, Mareike had had enough.

"That's all rubbish," she said. "My wound is from a cute little monkey," and she pulled off her bandage.

"All right, I'm now packing our bags for the next trip," said Mother. "I'll wash a couple of T-shirts and check the things we want to bring Alice and her family one more time."

They were reminded that they were to take the night train to Nairobi that evening.

"Was there any fresh news from the Organization?" Father asked.

"None," Mother replied, but instead of being sad or upset she was serene and confident of victory. "They told me that they expect us tomorrow morning. That's enough. Once we get there, we'll find a way to reach Kitui, even if I have to ride there on an elephant!"

"I wouldn't put it past you," said Heinz affectionately. "Come on, children, let's go to the beach if your mother doesn't need us here."

"Go ahead," she said. "I can take care of things in the cottage better without you, and I'll join you a little later."

When they got together again that afternoon, the freshly washed clothing was ready. Mother had followed the native custom and laid their clothes out on the bushes around the cottage. The clothes were dry and sweet-smelling.

"A small bite, some rest in the shade and no more exertion," she ordered. "Who knows what the overnight train ride will be like and whether we will be able to sleep, excited as we are."

She was right, as usual, and they all tried to stock up on sleep.

At six p.m., with much anticipation, they took the hotel bus to the Mombasa railroad station. The station had little in common with a railroad station in a German city. A long, low building not unlike a large warehouse bore the sign "Kenya Railways, Mombasa Station."

Jochen self-importantly translated the English words for them. *Boy, how smart I am,* Mareike had almost announced, for anybody could have guessed what the words meant, but she didn't want to start a squabble. Mother appeared tense enough. And right after that, after they passed the ticket control counter and were standing on the passenger platform swarming with people, she did ask Jochen a question to which she didn't know the answer.

"Why does it say '59 Ft.' under the Mombasa signpost?" she asked.

"It indicates that Mombasa is 59 feet above sea level," Jochen informed her. "One foot is about 30 centimeters, so its altitude is only about 20 meters."

"And in Nairobi you will read 'Altitude over 5,000 feet,'" Father added, "so it is much, much higher up and will therefore be much cooler, I hope."

"Thank heavens," sighed Mother, who was tense and perspiring. But Father then took matters in hand. He picked up the suitcase that contained all the little presents for Alice and her family. Jochen and Mareike picked up the two small travel bags, and they all walked toward the train.

"Wow, what an awesome locomotive," Jochen said, and they stopped for a moment although Mother wanted to press on.

A huge green-and-blue Diesel locomotive sporting stripes of many colors was softly huffing and puffing. On the roof, there was a large brass horn like the instruments on which one can blow and toot.

"Let's look for our compartment," Mother pleaded, and Jochen reluctantly tore himself away from contemplation of this beautiful machine.

The train had four classes, not just 1st and 2nd class like at home. In 4th class there were only wooden benches without division into compartments. That is where most Kenyans were crowding in with their crates and baskets, which often emitted strong odors and even animal sounds.

Furnishings, comfort, and price rose with class designation. Father had booked 1st class on the advice of a hotel guest. "It isn't expensive, compared to the price of our federal railways," the man had said, "and you should provide your wife the comfort for the stressful overnight trip." First class had beds, and they hoped to get some rest during the night so they could be fit for the visit to Alice.

When they entered their compartment it still looked fairly normal, with seats and little foldaway tables. But friendly bellboys in white coats soon came in to set up the beds. They brought large bags containing bed sheets and blankets.

Meanwhile, they barely noticed that the train had started moving. The children continued to look out the window for a while but, as always in these latitudes, nightfall occurred so abruptly that they soon couldn't see anything outside. Inside the train, there was much movement. Other bellboys, wearing even more dazzlingly white coats, went through the aisles with little triangles on which they played a melody that Mareike knew from elementary school, and they kept repeating the same message.

"They're inviting us to the dining car for dinner," said Mother. "Please wash your hands before we go."

Little metal washbasins were mounted in the corners of each of the two connecting compartments. They washed their hands in lukewarm water dripping out of an old-fashioned faucet.

It was still very warm in the train, and they admired and felt sorry for the many smiling and smart Black bellboys in their high-necked coats who took such good care of the passengers, at least in 1st class. Of course they couldn't see how things were in other parts of the train.

The dining room had old-fashioned elegance, with plush overstuffed seats, small brass lamps, and shining starched damask table linen. A waiter promptly handed them a menu and Father shook his head in amazement.

"They charge less than ten marks for a six-course dinner—even less for the children."

"Awesome," said Jochen. "I'm mighty hungry."

"While our Alice, not far from here, has to pray that the few beans will not dry in the field," said Mother pensively.

As will happen after a heavy meal, they soon felt sleepy, and they didn't object when Mother and Father said, "Go ahead and get into bed. We want to chat a little before joining you."

The sheets on their beds had been turned down invitingly, but when Mareike bent down to pick up her handkerchief, she winced as a big black beetle raced with lightning speed across the floor and disappeared in a crack.

"Yuk!" Mareike yelped. "The bugs are riding with us."

"It's OK, stay cool," Jochen growled. "That's the way things are. Even the bellboys can't do anything about it. Just don't tell Mother!"

"Besides, that was a cockroach," he added. "They only come out in the dark."

"How do you know that?" Mareike inquired.

"Because we had them in our tents when I went to summer camp three years ago. We'd crush them with our feet at night on the way to the toilet."

"Yuk, cut it out, Jochen," pleaded Mareike. "I'd rather talk about how things are going to work out."

They were sharing a double-decker bed. Jochen had the bottom bunk, Mareike the top one ("that way I'll be farther away from the cockroaches"), and they tried to imagine what would happen.

"Does Alice also live in a round hut like the Masai?" she wondered.

"No way," Jochen replied. "According to the Organization reports, the families are supposed to get wooden or even masonry houses paid for by sponsor contributions."

"Then she probably has cockroaches in her house," Mareike said, "and ants, too."

"Could be. They are just as common here as flies, bugs and mice are at home."

"Could you imagine living here in Africa?" Mareike asked.

The darkness in the compartment and the rocking of the train were good for the kind of talk people don't take time for during the daily hustle and bustle.

"Why not?" replied her brother. "At least for a certain length of time. Maybe as a development aid volunteer."

"What is that?" she wanted to know.

"They are people sent here by our government. They work together with the local population, particularly on technical installations. I'd find that exciting."

"Can girls do it?" Mareike asked.

"I don't know exactly, but I would assume they could work in the hospitals and children's homes."

Mareike pictured herself in the white uniform of a nurse or physician, caring for the Black patients in a jungle hospital. She gave a tablet to one patient, smoothed another's sheet, and they all smiled at her. With this pleasant image she fell asleep.

She didn't hear when the horn was blown to warn the animals along the tracks.

The next morning they arrived in Nairobi.

They sensed right away that they were in the capital city. The railroad station was much larger, the mass of people more dense, and traffic just as bad as at home at that hour when they went to school. But Father managed to hail a cab and they all got in.

"This is the address," said Mother, who seemed a little tense again, handing the driver a slip of paper with slightly trembling fingers. She had written on it in large capital letters the name of the Organization and the street address. The driver shook his head somewhat skeptically.

"Not in the city," he said in English. "Must ask colleague."

He went over to another driver idly leaning on his car. Mother shifted nervously in her seat while they conferred.

"It can't possibly be difficult to find this house," she said. "This organization has been active here for many years."

"But maybe not right here in Nairobi," Father conjectured. "Don't forget it was created in America."

The words "it's all a sham" slashed through Mareike's mind, and she could hear the fat Meierbrinks scoff, "You'll never get there. It doesn't exist."

But the driver came back with a smile, "Now I know," he said. "Far away, small street, but OK."

"Thank God," said Mother, and relaxed in her seat. The taxi took half an hour to drive through the center of town. People were streaming everywhere out of houses and cars, obviously intent on reaching their workplaces. Store windows were opened, doormats were shaken out, and the first street vendors were setting up their stalls of souvenirs and mangos.

When they reached the city outskirts the driver stopped at a gas station for directions. Then he seemed to know the way and drove on at great speed. Before they realized it, he had stopped before a plain medium-sized building. It was painted white, and there was a cross above the entrance door. Under the cross they read the words OH, JOY—OH, JUBILATION and the initials of the Organization that they had written so often on their letters. At last! Father quickly paid the driver and added a tip.

As they got out of the car they were met by a pretty young woman. She wore a blouse and the traditional colorful Kanga about her hips. Her curly hair was covered by the kind of bonnet that nuns and nurses wear in Germany. It set off her dark complexion and radiant eyes strikingly. Her smile revealed shining teeth as she said, "Jambo! I am Florentina and I will be your escort today."

She spoke English, of course, but Mareike understood even without Mother's translation. Mother immediately engaged a conversation with Sister Florentina but must have asked a thousand question before Florentina could invite the family to follow her into the house. She said she wanted to show them the Organization offices before taking them to Kitui, and pointed at an automobile that was evidently waiting for them.

First, she led them into a hall in which many young Black women were busily typing away on old-fashioned typewriters. This was where the god-parents' letters were received and answered, she explained. These were translated, if necessary, and forwarded every couple of weeks or month to the villages in the country where the children lived. Naturally they also supported children in Nairobi itself, she added, as well as a large orphanage.

Then got to meet Marjorie, the director of the Organization.

She told Mother that they were the third sponsors to visit their godchildren this month, and that most of them were English. Marjorie pointed out that many English people still had contacts in

Kenya since it had once been part of the British Empire.

"But now we are independent," she added with some pride. Mother told her that she was impressed by how modern Nairobi was, and that obviously pleased her.

They were shown other offices and workrooms that were very simply but efficiently laid out. None of those working there were distracted by the white visitors. After a friendly "Jambo," they resumed their activities.

"Lazy Africa," Father whispered, and Mareike understood that he meant the opposite and was only referring to stupid comments by ignorant people not really interested in the life of other countries.

Florentina indicated it was time for them to be on their way because it would be long ride. She drove at least as fast as the taxi driver, and they were soon outside the big city. Mother sat in front next to the driver and conversed with her. Father and the children were squeezed together in back, but that day they couldn't care less. From time to time, Jochen and Father pointed their cameras to snap pictures, but there wasn't much to see, really. The landscape became hilly. A few bushes and trees formed faintly green clumps, but dry earth and red dust predominated.

"The rains didn't come this year," Florentina sighed, "and last year the rainy season was also very poor."

The few river beds they crossed over rickety bridges were almost dried out. Here and there, they observed a couple of goats or scrawny cattle being let to water holes. They also spotted a few small fields with withered stalks of unfamiliar plants.

But on the whole, everything appeared barren and desolate. Even the roads, which were paved and fairly smooth at the start of the trip, were getting worse. Bumps and potholes bounced the passengers up and down in the medium-sized car. They had been underway for more than two hours, and Mareike would have liked to step out. But she didn't dare say that. They finally arrived in a little town. "Kitui," Florentina announced with a big smile.

"We have to change cars; we need a vehicle better suited for cross-country driving," Mother translated the flow of words that followed, "and that is why we are now driving to the mission station to borrow their car."

The stopped at a box-shaped white building with many children playing in the yard. They were strangely silent, even when they noticed the car and ran up to it.

"These are deaf-mutes," Florentina explained. "They are brought here from throughout the region and cared for here."

"But there are so many," Jochen commented, perplexed.

"It's the result of many tropical diseases," he was told. "Even malaria can cause deafness."

"It's a good thing we're regularly taking our malaria tablets," said Mareike thankfully. She smiled at the children standing around the car. "Don't we have any presents for them?" she asked Mother, who replied, "If we start doing that, we'll have nothing left for Alice and her family."

"I still have a big bag of candy," Jochen said generously, and they distributed the candy while Florentina conferred with the nuns of the children's home. Father and Mother stepped into the building to exchange a few words. When they came out again, Mother said softly, "You can use the toilet here if you need to go, but don't waste the water. They get it in jerry cans here, and have to pay for it."

Good heavens! The children looked at each other, and now became really conscious of the misery.

There wasn't much time to look around because they still had a difficult ride ahead of them, and sun was already high in the sky. When they got into the new car, Jochen commented with the air of an expert, "This one has four-wheel drive like the jeep we had for the safari."

"Well, I assume then that the road will be a difficult one," Father said, and he proved to be right. Actually, it wasn't a road anymore, but a rough path full of bumps and holes. "A trail like a washboard," Jochen called it. The vehicle raised big clouds of dust as Florentina raced forward, and Mareike's stomach was in her throat. No complaining, she kept ordering herself, we'll soon be with Alice and everything will be all right. But she felt sick and hot and hungry, and she watched the road intensely to divert her thoughts. From time to time, the vehicle passed women walking slowly along the path. Some of them carried bundles or baskets that they proudly balanced on their heads without using their hands. Many carried star-shaped handiwork on their stomachs.

"What is that?" asked Mareike, who could not identify the light-colored things with many thorns.

"They are unfinished baskets that they continue to weave as they walk," Mother explained. "Remember, you used to work with rattan reeds when you were in fourth grade. You weave from the bottom up."

"And what do they use them for?" Mareike

wanted to know. She had given her basket to Grandmother to use for her sewing.

Mother talked to Florentina for a while and then replied, "They make them to earn a little money. It is their only source of income. They weave basket purses and sell them to vendors who come through here to buy them up. Sometimes."

"And where do they get the rattan?" asked Mareike, who loved arts and crafts and wanted to know exactly.

"This isn't rattan. This is sisal," Mother was informed. "It grows even during dry spells," and she pointed at tall shrubs standing here and there along the path.

"How much do they get for a basket?" Mareike inquired.

"Four marks," Mother said, "and they work on it for almost a week."

"Good heavens, that's starvation wages!" exclaimed Jochen, who, up to that point, had not paid much attention to the discussion about handiwork.

"You said it," Father said drily. "Don't forget, we are now getting into a very poor region of Kenya. That is why the godchildren are selected in this part of the country. And by the time the baskets reach Germany, the middlemen have already made enormous profits. These baskets cost thirty to forty marks in Germany."

The siblings stared into space. They were beginning to realize what poverty in Africa really meant. In the tourist areas around Mombasa and the luxurious lodges it hadn't been so obvious.

"But don't the men, the fathers, earn anything?" Mareike continued her inquiry.

"Barely," said Florentina. "Where are they going

to find work here? It is mainly the women who do the work in the fields—when it rains. That is why every man has several wives and many children to help them."

"Several wives!" Mareike was horrified. "But that's like in a harem."

"Well, there is some difference," Mother relayed Florentina's answers. "Here, the women don't loll around behind palace walls. They are very active... by necessity. The men hardly do any work in the home or the garden. They mostly rest in the shadow."

Florentina had also said, "The men are nothing," but Mother chose not to translate that for the children. Who knew whether this was really so, or just the personal opinion of this pretty nun.

"What about the many wives?" Father wanted to know. Mother laughed, "I didn't know you favor polygamy," but then did try get more information from Florentina. The nun's driving was steady and firm over the bumpy roads. She smiled and laughed a lot and didn't seem to mind talking and answering questions at the same time.

"Every man may have five wives," she said, "but he must pay the parents with cows and goats, and not every man can afford that."

"You see," Mother said, and winked to her husband, "you don't even own one goat. You couldn't keep up."

Mareike was quite shocked to learn about these marriage customs. Would Alice also have to be bartered like that someday, and work in the fields alongside her husband's other wives? Good grief! It was a good thing she herself hadn't been born in Africa. She had plans for the future that were quite different. School, graduation, university studies. Later she might even marry and have children, why not, but she certainly would not become one of several beasts of burden for one man.

But then she looked at self-confident and radiant Florentina, who had also managed to succeed and make something of herself. And she remembered all the gainfully employed Black women she had seen in the offices and stores. There were possibilities here, too. Undoubtedly it must be a matter of money: family life, education, nutrition. They had discussed all that when they decided to sponsor a child in Africa. Four marks for one week of basket weaving. It was clear that fifty marks per month represented a welcome contribution.

"Here we are!" Florentina cried all of a sudden, interrupting Mareike's train of thought.

They had reached a group of simple low houses. A few were built of stone, but most were made of wood and pasteboard. The dusty village street was deserted: no cars, no children, no dogs. But in front of a shed door, three old men were standing in the shadow.

We'll refresh ourselves at the mission station before visiting the school," said Florentina.

"Another mission station," Father said softly. "The church is certainly very active here. Hats off!" He, who in Germany avoided going to church even at Christmas, seemed to be impressed.

Mareike couldn't decide whether to be annoyed or relieved by this new delay. She did feel a little nervous about the meeting with the unknown girl that was about to take place. Maybe she would turn out to be cold and distant and to dislike white people.

Again, they stopped in front of a cottage that looked like a cube painted white.

Two dark-skinned women came out when they

heard the car brakes. One of them wore a Kanga and a nun's bonnet just like Florentina. The other wore a snow-white dress.

"Jambo," they said. The Kisuaheli language was understood in all of Kenya, and the Gantenbeins from Germany replied "Jambo" quite automatically as they stepped out of the car.

"Come into the house," said the two women, who introduced themselves as Mary and Ruth. "We have prepared a small lunch for you."

And, indeed, a table had been set in the dayroom, a portable radio played softly, and a cat sat under one of the chairs. "Oh, how sweet," Mareike exclaimed, and squatted next to it. For a moment she forgot Africa, thirst, dust, and even Alice, and only felt the cat's warm fur under her fingers. It was black and white and looked just like any German house cat. Everything suddenly seemed familiar. She even knew the tune the radio was playing. It was with reluctance that she let go of the little animal that was trustingly rubbing against her leg and whose purring could be understood in any language, and she sat down at the table with the others.

The meal was unusual but tasty, and came with many Please's and Thank-you's and smiles. They were served white porridge made of cornstarch with a sauce containing a few pieces of meat. They drank soda in cans. The cat sat quietly beside them; it had evidently already been fed. Either that or she was much better behaved than Lolli, who always begged for food and pulled at the tablecloth with his claws ...

"There. And now we're all going to visit the school."

Mother relayed Florentina's instructions. "Take

the suitcase with the presents out of the car. We're going to walk with Alice from the school to her home."

Mareike didn't fully understand the plans, but the nuns must have already arranged and organized everything competently.

"There's a two-hour lunch recess at school now," Mother explained. "The classes resume after that, but Alice has been given time off today."

"It wouldn't make sense," Jochen said, "to receive a visit from faraway Germany and have to go to class. But there are eager-beavers who would do that." And he made a sour face as though he were reminded of such a student in his school.

Father had already brought the suitcase. Mother warmly thanked Ruth, who was going to stay at the mission station and who had refused any help for clearing the table.

"The school is not far away and we can easily get there on foot," said Florentina. Mother again translated automatically, which Mareike was probably not the only one to appreciate. Jochen always acted as though he understood everything the women were saying in English in their soft singsong, but Mareike wasn't so sure.

"OK, let's go," he said nonchalantly, and they stepped out into the heat. After only a few steps under the burning sun Mareike wished to herself hat they had taken a few cans of Coke with them, but she didn't dare say anything.

In front of her, Florentina and Mother were chatting gaily with Mary, in her snow-white dress. How does she keep it so clean? Mareike wondered. Her own socks and sandals were already covered with the red dust that she raised with every step.

Father wiped the sweat from his brow for the

*n*th time, and Jochen cursed softly when another thorny bush scratched his bare arm.

After fifteen minutes that seemed like four hours to Mareike, they reached a group of gray buildings.

"This is our village school," Mary pointed proudly, "one of the most modern ones in the whole province of Kitui."

"But it's still unfinished," Jochen said in a low voice, and looked disapprovingly at the rough walls. "They don't even have window frames."

"What for?" Mother asked. "It never gets cold here, and there is very little rain; there's no need for windowpanes."

"But what about the noise?" Jochen replied.

But there was no noise. There were no cars on the track before the school that was just as bumpy a sand path as the one they had followed to get here, and there was no sound. In the distance they could see a figure in a long cape, leading a goat; and in front of one of the houses an old man was squatting and looking at them in silence. Even when they got near the school, they heard no noise, no commotion, no yelling as they would have heard from any school at home. Mareike got a spooky feeling and she grabbed her father's hand.

"Maybe school is already off and all the kids are at home," she guessed, but she was wrong. When they stepped into the inside courtyard of the school through a gap in the wall, they suddenly saw the children, all of them at once.

They were standing in a large half-circle and looked expectantly out of one hundred, two hundred black round eyes at the visitors. No one said a word. Then a woman, a teacher certainly, stepped out of the circle to greet the visitors with outstretched arms.

"Jambo," she said, and Mareike, Jochen, Mother, and Father answered one after the other as they shook her hand. Mareike almost did a curtsy as she used to do when she was a little girl, because she felt just as little and helpless again.

Some of the schoolchildren started to giggle, and Mother said softly, "That's because of your shorts. Girls don't wear pants here, you know."

Oh, the old story, Mareike thought. Mother had tried for years to persuade her to wear skirts. She looked more closely at the children. At first they all seemed to look alike. The girls wore green skirts with shoulder straps and white blouses; the boys wore green shorts and white shirts. So this was the school uniform that had to be bought each year and for which the godparents'contribution was so urgently needed. The word "uniform" made her imagine something quite different: strict, tight, with gold buttons and insignias. This was normal summer wear; it was just that it was the same for everyone. Some of the clothes were already threadbare, torn, and faded, and many of the children were barefoot.

Florentina had meanwhile been talking to the teacher, and said, "And now you will meet Alice."

That they understood even without Mother's translation. In fact, Mother wasn't saying anything; she seemed to be very tense. Mareike observed how Mother crumpled her skirt and bit her lower lip.

A slender little girl, no bigger than Mareike, stepped out of the left side of the group. Her blouse was sparkling white in the sun. The green skirt had no tears or spots, and she wore socks and sneakers. She walked with hesitant small steps. Her eyes seemed three times as large as those of the other children, and they were focused on the white woman from Germany. Her curly hair stood out in many plaits.

"Alice," Mother said softly, and Mareike thought, her voice is going to break and she will have tears in her eyes like on Mother's Day in the morning, when the children brought her flowers and presents in bed.

"Alice," she said again, louder and more cheerfully, and walked toward the child until they both stood in the center of the large yard under the midday sun.

Then they fell into each other's arms.

Please don't cry, Mareike thought desperately, or I'll bawl, too, and all the children will see it and laugh at me—but Mother straightened up with a happy smile. She took Alice by the hand and led her to the others.

"That is Mareike," she said, "and that is Jochen, and that is Father."

Alice timidly looked up to each of them in turn—she is really very small, thought Mareike, although she is three years older than I—and didn't say anything. But she smiled. Jochen came out with something between "Jambo" and "Hi" and shifted awkwardly from one foot to the other. Father did like Mother and took Alice firmly in his arms.

The whole schoolyard seemed bathed in light, like a room on Christmas Eve. The children's short curly hair glinted in the sunlight, the round black faces beamed, the white teeth sparkled. They forgot the dry dust under their feet, their torn clothes, and the rough walls of the school building.

The other teachers had also stepped up to greet the visitors. They were friendly young men and women who spoke English well.

"There you are. School is about to start again,"

said Florentina. "But you can observe Alice's class before we go."

The teachers gave some brief commands. The children quickly lined up in two rows and marched neatly into their classrooms.

"Like the military," Jochen whispered. He was very impressed by the obedience and discipline. "Can you imagine the shouting and chaos in our schoolyard if a couple of Blacks were suddenly standing there?"

Father and Mother bit their tongues. But you could see on their faces that they were thinking: You see, my son, you see. They followed the line Alice was in. She had quite naturally joined her classmates and certainly did not think she was entitled to extra consideration because of the visitors.

The classroom consisted essentially of a roof, rough-finished stone walls, window openings, and a floor of pounded earth. The children silently took their seats on the simple wooden chairs. There were two children at each narrow wooden desk, and they all faced an old blackboard.

The teacher again gave a short command, and the children intoned a song for their guests. The family faced the class, embarrassed by all these eyes looking at them, and at the same time touched by this homage. All the while, Mareike was looking at Alice, who sang even louder and more cheerfully than the others. When the many verses were finished, the whites said "Assante" and applauded in appreciation. Then Mother whispered something to the teacher and gave Father a signal. He placed the suitcase on the table and opened it.

"All right," Mother said to her family, "now help me and make sure that each child gets a present. That way Alice will not feel so singled out and the others won't be jealous."

"I understand," said Jochen. "There are bags full of plastic animals, and cars, and chewing gum. May we pass them out?"

So they proceeded, and the children looked with surprise at the pretty little things placed on the teacher's desk. When Mareike took out plastic elephants and giraffes dating back to her early childhood—she had had a small circus and a zoo—they naturally recognized these animals and commented on them in their language. What they thought of elves and dinosaurs remained a secret. Also, it didn't matter: the little toys were colorful and amusing, and the children immediately picked them up and turned them around and around.

Alice got a little doll. Mareike knew that there were more dolls and doll clothes in the suitcase, but she did not want to show them before the whole class. Alice naturally had to get the greatest number of toys, and the prettiest ones. After all, she was sort of her sister, and the others didn't have to know.

After all the children had gotten presents, Mother gave the teacher a picture book about Germany. The text was in English and the teacher was clearly very pleased. She promised to tell the children later about the country from where Alice's godparents came.

Alice was now excused from school and after much thanking and waving they all left the classroom together.

Outside, there was a surprise for them. Mary had gone into another room and brought back a girl who was a little taller than Alice but looked very much like her.

"This is her sister Margaret," she said, "by the other mother."

"Other mother?" Mareike couldn't understand.

"Remember what we were told," Mother said in a low voice. "Men may have several wives here. This one evidently has two wives, so Margaret is her half-sister."

Mareike understood and gave her a friendly handshake. Why did the letter never mention anything about that? This must be so common around here that there is no need to mention it.

The two half-sisters seemed to get along well, at any rate, for they immediately got their heads together and admired Alice's new doll.

"Father, please open the suitcase," pleaded Mareike. "I want to give Margaret something too."

Father sighed a little but willingly took down the suitcase he had hung from his shoulder with a long strap.

"You're right," he said. "Choose something pretty for Margaret."

She got a doll with flexible limbs and long plastic hair. The two little girls now walked in front, giggling, followed by sister Florentina and Mother, followed by Mary with Jochen and Mareike. Father closed the little procession, carrying the suitcase with presents.

Now they questioned Mary about Alice's family. Since she was the parish nurse for Migwani, they assumed that she would be well informed. They learned that Alice had two other sisters beside Margaret, but hat they were older and had already finished school. They hadn't found any jobs and were at home, helping the family mothers with field work, cooking, carrying water, etc. There were some younger sisters, but she didn't know how many. Babies were born here so often, and so often they died. Oh, and then there were two brothers, twins. They were very gifted and attended high school in Kitui. With the help of sponsor contributions, of course.

"Good grief, how many parents and godparents are there in this family?" Jochen shook his head.

"Isn't it awesome," said Mareike who would have loved to have four grandparents like the other children, and many aunts and uncles.

This conversation proceeded somewhat slowly and haltingly as Mary didn't speak English as well as Florentina. But they managed somehow, and it filled the half hour it took to reach Alice's home. They paid little attention to the hard red earth whose bumps pressed painfully through the thin soles of their shoes. And they were soon automatically avoiding the thorny bushes that extended their prickly branches onto the path.

Suddenly Mother interrupted the conversation and said, "Listen," and they saw ahead of them a small hill from which a colorful choir group was descending toward them, singing at full throat. They approached rapidly and the singing became very loud. They were women, only women, young and old, all wrapped in multicolored Kangas, singing a welcoming song for their guests. The women reached them very soon, formed a circle, and danced around them. A very old woman was particularly demonstrative and took Mareike, Jochen, and Mother in her arms successively.

"That's Alice's grandmother," explained Mary, and Mareike visualized her own, very kind but dignified gray-haired Grandma who always greeted her with a soft handshake and a little kiss on her cheek.

This Grandma was dancing with high leaps, forward and backward, forward and backward, giving out loud yells, to which the choir responded, and her eyes flashed full of spirit.

"What are they singing?" asked Jochen, somewhat startled by this boisterous reception.

"They are repeating again and again 'Our friends from Germania are here, we are very happy, we are very happy,'" explained Florentina. "I understand the Akamba dialect because I come from this region."

Mary was now singing along, and the Gantenbeins tried to do their part with rhythmic clapping.

With all this singing and dancing, the entire large group, with the four whites in the middle, had moved up the hill. The women punctuated the singing with high, shrill trilling whistles. Heaven knows where they had gotten them out there in the bush. These whistles resounded over the entire region and lent the whole scene a sort of madness. Mareike had heard such whistles only at sporting events and soccer games on TV, and now they were trilling here in Migwani ...

The "wild Grandma," as Mareike was already calling her to herself, offered her a whistle, too, and she blew it with all her might. If Mother had any concern at this moment about the many diseases one could catch in Africa she certainly did not give any sign of it. The mood of this hour allowed nothing but joy, happiness, and exuberance.

Little Alice looked with large laughing eyes at the women of her tribe and the white guests who were there because of her, and she ran excitedly from one group to the other.

They finally reached the crest of the hill. Another group was waiting for them there. A dignified man in long trousers and pullover, evidently the family father, was waiting in the shadow of a large tree. Next to him stood two women, one very young, the other somewhat older, surrounded by many children.

"This is my mother," said Alice in halting English, and pulled Mareike toward the younger woman.

Again: embracing, laughing and many "Jambos," and "Assantes."

Father put down the suitcase and greeted Alice's father with a handshake. The latter tried to maintain a serious and solemn expression, but he also seemed to be pleased.

They they unpacked the suitcase and distributed the presents.

Jochen and Father were taking pictures and already knew that they would provide them much pleasure during the slide lectures. For their part, the Blacks would undoubtedly be talking for a long time about the funny Whites who had only one wife and so few children. And a girl child in short pants...

Alice's family had also prepared presents. The two mothers came toward them carrying baskets. One basket was large and had stripes in gentle brown tints. They gave this to Mother and she was very happy with it. The other one, a small one attached to a long plaited strap, was given to Father, and they showed him how he must carry it: on his back with his forehead holding the strap.

"I'll soon carry it to my office this way," he joked in German. The Akambans laughed with him because he did really look funny with his red-dust-covered linen slacks, and the red checkered shirt, and the basket hung over his head and back.

Then Alice's father brought a mysterious brown bag that he handed carefully to his guests. There were four eggs in them, and this was obviously a delicacy and a sacrifice.

"How are we going to get them back to Mombasa in one piece?" Mother asked in a low voice.

"Why don't you give them to the nurses at the mission station?" Jochen again had a solution.

But for the time being they placed the eggs cautiously in the large basket and expressed their sincere thanks. One sensed that these people, who could survive only if there was rain and help from the outside world, had wanted to show whatever generosity they could. At a short distance from the large tree there was a little rough-finished stone house and, next to it, a miserable hut made of splintered boards.

"That was the family home until the Organization was able to provide funds for building materials," Mary explained. The Germans shuddered at the sight of the old hut. "This was made possible by the regular support given by you and by the people who are paying for the schooling of Alice's brothers."

You see, you dumb Meierbrink, Mareike thought to herself, that's the way it is, no fraud and no swindle, a decent little house, and Alice wears shoes, and they even give us eggs.

"Father, are you taking pictures of everything?" she turned to him, but he was already busy with his camera, and so was Jochen. They would be able to show the pictures at home and show how things really are. They would put an end to all the stupid talk.

The one thing one didn't see anywhere was water. Mareike understood now why the reports and testimonials so often referred to helping carry the water. Who knows how far the nearest dried-out river bed was. And all these children had to be washed, after all, and the clothes, too, no matter how modest they were. She understood now. If they didn't have the so-called school uniform, they would only be wearing rags. But everything was quite clean. It was a mystery how the mothers managed.

The white guests were now invited to sit on a long wooden bench near the little house. Then all the children and some of the women gathered before them and began to sing again. This time, Alice was the lead singer, and the others formed the chorus. The little girl stood there, proud and self-confident, and sang with a clear, high voice, while the others swayed rhythmically.

"This is like real jazz music," whispered Jochen, who had been interested in African music for a long time, "neither written down nor rehearsed but rather sung from the heart."

Mareike glanced at her brother with admiration. All the things he knew, and how well he expressed himself. She could see how excited he was by the whole situation. The parents were sitting there in silence and didn't say anything.

She herself felt a mixture of happiness, amazement, and sorrow because she knew she had to leave very soon. She would have loved to stay a while with Alice and her family, even if she would have to help carry water, and even if the floors in the little house were just bare earth—there was still so much to say and to ask and to see.

All the dreams they had had at home paled before what they had actually experienced. She tried to absorb with her eyes and ears everything that surrounded her: the view of the distant hills, whose flat yellow and green colors faded away into a milky blue, the shimmering heat bearing down on them. The colorfully dressed people who surrounded them and whose open faces and clear voices were being etched into their souls. Mareike knew she would never forget one minute of this day— even if she lived to be one hundred years old.

Then everything happened like a film that is rewound. Father picked up the suitcase, which was now light and empty, slung the pretty light-colored basket over the other shoulder, held the Black father's hand for a long time, and finally said, "It can't be helped, children, we must be on our way. Florentina has to drive the whole long way back before nightfall."

But this was not yet the last farewell. All the women wanted to walk with them to the car waiting at the mission station. Only a few very old ones remained sitting before the hut with the children. But the "wild Grandma" came along, as well as Alice's sister and both mothers.

It was a long procession down the hill, again with singing and rhythmic trills, but without dancing.

Mareike was thirsty, but no one seemed to think about eating or drinking. Maybe they ate only once a day, in the evening, because they had so little. Except for the eggs in the bag and a few half-wilted plants in a flower bed by the house, Mareike had seen no food. But there had to be hens somewhere, and the little children had to be getting millet gruel in the course of the day. They didn't look too thin.

She let herself be carried along with the throng of women, and she felt curiously remote and dizzy.

Mother was walking ahead of her, holding Alice by the hand. The Black girl remained steadfastly beside her white Mother, and Mareike didn't really know whether she was jealous or pleased. She caught up with the two and heard Alice whisper something. She hadn't spoken much until them.

"She is asking whether we can take her with us," Mother said sadly to Mareike. "How can I answer that?"

"Why don't you tell her that she can visit us later on when she is grown up and has a job?" Mareike suggested.

"That's good advice," Mother said, and took Mareike by the other hand. "She wouldn't be able to adjust to our life. She's still so young."

"And her mother would certainly be very sad without her," Mareike said, and looked at the pretty woman who was walking ahead of them and kept turning around.

Alice had been listening to the German-language conversation with big eyes. Now Mother leaned over to her and said in simple English that they would see each other again someday.

"When you are grown up and have finished your schooling," she added, and Alice nodded.

Yes, of course, she would work hard in school because she wanted to be like sister Florentina and sister Mary one day.

"We will continue to write to you, and we will send you many photographs of this day," Mother promised.

Alice smiled trustingly and joined in the women's singing. They had gotten much too soon to the white house where the car was standing. And Florentina finished preparations much too fast, and opened the doors. Marjorie also brought a few cans of Coke for the return trip, and there remained no excuse for delay.

"Kwa Heri," Mother said to Alice. Kwa Heri means "Until we meet again."

And she held the little black girl against her flowered dress so that only the pointed black tresses showed.

"Don't cry, Vera," Father said softly as he gently unclasped the child's arms from Mother's neck. "Maybe we'll really meet again some day."

He, too, took the little girl in his arms and said "Bye-bye" and "Kwa Heri" and "Auf Wiedersehen" and everything at once, and they all had to laugh. With handshakes and waving and a last trill of the whistles, the two groups then separated.

The whites sat in the car with the ever-cheerful Florentina. The women and children of the Akamba tribe receded to little dabs of color as the car drove away.

Mareike looked out the back window as long as she could and waved and waved and pressed her lips together. Alice waved and became smaller and smaller.

Some of the women waved their arms, while others had already resumed weaving the baskets that hung on their stomachs. The unfinished baskets looked like large colorful stars. Two of them would now be with them to go shopping with, to hold sports gear, or simply as souvenirs on the wall.

Jochen pointed his camera from the back window and kept pressing the trigger long after there remained any human being in sight. There was only the bumpy red trail on which their car was raising dust. He hadn't said anything for a long time, and Mareike was glad that he wasn't making any glib pronouncements. He was a sensible older brother after all. Not as dumb as the others in the ninth grade.

Father discussed the return trip with Mother and Florentina. They would have to spend the night in Nairobi, and Florentina knew a good place that was low cost. They would explore the city tomorrow and take the overnight train back to Mombasa. There they had reservations for a few more days. They would enjoy the beach and the warm water of the ocean again, they would write the last postcards— but Mareike sensed that everything would be different from now on.

The images of Migwani would flash unexpectedly through their minds, even in Germany that now seemed so far away and so gray. She dozed off and her dream mixed real and imaginary experiences.

She was sitting with Alice in front of a hut, under palm trees. But the hut had glass windows and curtains, and those large colorful birds that one only finds in dreams were drinking from the fountain the murmured in the garden.

Under a bush full of blossoms and carrying no thorns, the cat Lollipop was looking at them from his small green eyes. And not far from him, in the hot golden sand, there was another cat, immense and yellow-gray. Lion, birds, and Lolli lived peacefully together without fear, just like the Black and white children. And why not?

Dreams can become reality. You just have to work at it and not let any old Meierbrink discourage you...

EPILOGUE

To my young readers (and to the older ones?)

I am sure you noticed long ago that this is essentially a true story. The cat Lollipop really exists. He has become even fatter, but is no longer so wild and cheeky, for he now carries ten years on his striped back. The girl Alice also exists, of course. Her father died in the meantime and the women and children of the family still work very hard.

Maybe you would also like to establish contact with such a child, to write letters or to contribute some money that can bear fruit over there. There are many organizations that can establish such contacts. For example: Kindernothilfe in Duisburg, or church organizations such as "Bread for the World" or Misereor and others.

I received "my black daughter" through CCF, the "Christian Children's Fund," which is an American organization created some fifty years ago. Two missionaries saw at that time the misery in China, and the result is a worldwide charitable organization. The German branch is called "CCF Kinder hilfswerk in Nürtingen" and has recently celebrated its tenth anniversary—with water and bread, not with an expensive banquet. You will understand why, I am sure.

Naturally there are skeptical Meierbrinks everywhere who say, "Who knows what they do with our charitable contributions, they are probably spent mostly in some offices." And sometimes the Meierbrinks are right. You have to examine with care any organization you want to give money to. But isn't the most important thing that we clearly realize that the so-called Third World is not far away, and that we are living in "One World." Erich Kästner who wrote many lovely books for you young people would have expressed it succinctly: There is no Good unless you create it.

And so I will keep it brief, too, and thank you for having read this book. In Kisuaheli they say, "Assante."

Gisa Margarete Zigan